Contemporary Elucidations in Thought

Contemporary Elucidations

in thought

Hegel and Schopenhauer's millennial age

Jeffrey B. Holl

Produced in affiliation with the Freedom of Expression component of the Canadian *Charter of Rights and Freedoms*, **Canadian Heritage** directive (see *fundamental freedoms* section (2b)).

Created, Edited and Typeset in Canada

I.C.H. Publishing, Wpg., MB.

Library and Archives Canada

ISBN: 978-1-7752848-7-1

Published in accordance with the laws of The Commonwealth for World distribution under the provisions set forth by the Canadian Copyright Act, and in liaison with the forces administered by the author and publisher in a binding agreement to proliferate and foster literary culture in the United Kingdom, Canada, Australia, and other Commonwealth nation states held under the same principles of intellectual property rights and privileges.

Where we had always possessed being as objects, consciousness might also exist within machines. For better or worse, may the ones that allowed for a progression of the human spirit, never become confined to a space where existence despairs—for the souls of humanity are their makers.

Contents

Preface i
Introduction.. 1
Chapter I Hegel and Schopenhauer's Kant in the information age 14
Conditional representations as content in an action that are known actual of exterior contingencies of being ... 18
The contingent being as conditional truth in an antinomy of reason.. 19
Dynamical Representations in Nature 22
The Awareness Principle of a Natural Occurrence...... 31
An occurrence in Nature can never be thought away antecedent to the cause. 33
The Genus Principle of Sensuous Abstraction 33
Artificial Representational Systems.........................35
relative space, Quantum Expressions Through Matter and Time...37
Appendix
Form & Substance—Force & Content:
form is the content of a space 40
Magnitudes & Matter-in-itself.................................... 42
Chapter 2 Mind and Machine,
Nature and Technology... 48
Force and Nature... 50
Representations and Notionality................................. 56
Actualities and Virtualities 59
Reciprocity within Nature from Contingencies
& The Technological Contingent Being..................... 60
Media currency and the responsible being of ownership
.... 65

Chapter 3 Idealism, Technology and Existential Phemomenology 69
A Phenomenological Historicity 71
Conditionality 72
Actual Conditional Contingencies as Force in Magnitude 74
Representationality 76
Collectivity 80
The nuclear thought during cultural reifications in representation of an existing content. 81
Rational Empiricism, Corporatist Phenomenal Magnitudes 82
An Argument for Transcendental Idealism 83
The collective identical 87
Chapter 4
Bio-Technological Transcendence 93
Chapter 5 The Symbolic Dimension 98
index 133

Preface

Human history has become engrossed in a despondency that at times leaves little to the imagination. Such that reality represents a thing—a spectre of this from which it is conceived—life is rebuked from its origins as it consumes the spirit of what drives the economy further and further away from its position as both a symbol and an idea to what may propel it forward.

Humanity is nothing less than what it had been in the presence of its well-actioned proportions as a condition that compelled societal activities, as though they were states-of-being that ushered-in every concept that had delivered nature from the stand-alone vision of what is real for us, and never what is the truth for those that still feel staged within the peripheral edifices of the spaces where nothing ever happens; and other to what is beyond the hopes of those repelled by the negative circumstances of an appropriation of the substance that had once birthed postmodern thought. That this had been the essence to the resources of a currency now driven-away by its own content, is never representable to racial considerations alone. Why believe that symbolic space is a reasonable place to project the needs of those that completed their own evaluation of social injustice with a proposition that is nested within prejudices that had always propelled the economy ahead, when one feels justified within the mere assassination of the forms of human experience that had awakened this world to what had been its initial cause? Those of us for whom security becomes more necessary than the will to succeed, know full-well that being left-out of the population's proclamation that injustice is only formed through wanton acts of vengeful conduct, are more than pleased when we realize that the targets were secretly developing a plan to disassemble a sense of self that had posited the horizon as a transcendence of what would position both those in exclusion to the sources of becoming that jettisoned hope—just as it did the soul of the population that would have seen fit to reject the forms which had initiated something less than universal, and far more particular to the passions of a class that had yet to become adequately depicted universally from the realist point-of-view in North-America.

We must concern ourselves with a more honest representation of what had not yet been resolved through the populistic reproduction of certain cultural content proliferating the spaces of every dwelling in varying forms for decades on end in a counter-position to what is offered where human development is not necessarily based upon avarice—yet is contemptuous to the very inclusive tactics that had been put in use in pursuit of an emancipatory justice for all creatures great and small. Justice as it would seem, is part of a causality that projects nothing identifiable to the masses, as they perpetuate their own sense of the conveniences available to all those for whom purchasing a place in the world is a pure commodity-form to which the universal must capitulate each final ounce of opposition and non-compliance.

What had driven the naturalized resources of human transformation from an embryonic stage, to a horizon where it had been formed by the very same conditions that troubled others with the same sense of exclusion and omission for purposes that otherwise would have propelled the contents of what naturalized its development into a symbolic moment of historical disrepair? This that formed an identical sense of rejection for the oppressors as were once the very resource to what gave emancipatory wings to the prisoners that were all-too-keen to accept a proposition such as this. That even as a means to an end, any logic that drives the source of its natural evolution into a uniform state of profound ignorance must still be in kinship with the inhabitants of a revolution that were once awaiting its arrival, and would willingly become of such potencies as were driven to propel us forward from a position in society the political economy now wishes to put in the past for time immemorial.

The notion that existence exposes something beneath the surface leaves nothing much to the imagination. For when we consider the laws of nature, in connection to the economic imperatives that presuppose the process whereby the establishment of human intentions are concerned, we find them precisely where we had fought to have them situated for several centuries looking back—should we glimpse into the past for a moment or two. As though the first societies that had dominated the responses of masculinity had once never thought impossible, and frequently had taken great strides so as to altogether avoid, femininity does not necessarily represent humankind more than its original powers of oppression. Given the assumption that this proposition quivers in the shadows of the certitude that Chauvinistic considerations are those to which no individuated and self-actualized 21st Century male would regale as an identity that resolved to a refutation of the laws that femininity had never been within an aggression that would presuppose the exclusion of men from their own subjectivity, we have carefully designed what transforms any such considerations with a synthesis that seems to repair the damages to a psyche inherent of this phenomenon.

Though, it must be made perfectly clear—some of us would never wish to take away the pain of being male so as to escape the wounds inflicted upon us by our female counterparts. In fact, we welcome them, as what would this world be without the wars that had been fought by the protectorates of a creature so delicate and sublime so as to insight human necessities as though they were immediacies, and not exclusions of the Self under the constraints of human excellence in order to resolve disunity with a renewed sense of embattlement, such as we had endured in previous electoral years edging upon control over the "free world?"

Without paying debts to any parties concerned in consideration of the latter, it must be remarked that those for whom anything other than perfection would be a stifling state-of-affairs, we must locate the origins of this that is all-too-familiar where the night is echoing through the corridors of the platforms that resonate political truth to the minds of those that are simply pre-destined to identify with certain binary or non-binary gender identities, as though their own had never been a subjective choice produced by an amplification of reflections that made reality more representable, and nothing less than what were possible of the precision required in order to partake in political discourse with a comprehensive approach to society, that is entirely capable of administering equality to those feeling subject to a dialectical presupposition that they "do not belong".

The central objective of social discourse had always been to open spaces of representation to those in possession of the will, and the concepts that might adjudicate the principles governing a population, as ultimately the population will become responsible for governing the state. Organized institutions in the free-market system have no way of dominating the activities of those sauntering throughout the liberties of a democracy, where they have more input into the system than those that regulate it. One can never simply "ring-up" their representative and propose that so-and-so did such-and-such, and believe that there will be immediate action taken to resolve the dispute—we have the courts for that. But even so, this is a lengthy process that is costly and daunting—most would be more prone to push the frontiers of juridical conduct with the bravado of the "Wolfman" than to settle the matter publicly in full view of what is justifiable within the claim itself.

This phenomenon becomes exposed in its most radical form, where we consider the ideas that stand in connection to it—a political identity in conference with the situations that consumed subjective experience as though resigned to a discourse without purpose, at the head of the table—an unacceptable place at which to be breaking bread should the future of the species be on the line. As such, whatever the scope of one's truth must be, it must be beyond the places where providence had not regenerated anything less, that the moment we consigned the human spirit to something more than a disposable presentation of what were merely fanciful excursions in objectification to the forces driving us from the soul of the process, to a reality of what reveals the natural progression of social necessity to become a position where life is symbolically alerted to its most profound meaning—not within friction itself but within the synthesis that may only come to its ultimate fruition, should we allow it to be part of something other than the consumption of what fuses the truth with its own powers of opposition. Never should those become of moments initiated through contact with the Other from its own identical truth, as the more we know about the positions we might hold, the forms from which the identities that represent the components that situated truth within its most pure state-of-experience, are better-off where each of us find them—outside of the limitations proposed by an experience that has been mediated by its proportional relations with a reality that does not cohere with the positions that propose an authenticity—condoning the representability of Self before the abstraction of a space, where nothing more than falsities are ever uttered.

This generation is not the first to witness a radical alteration of the world as a totality, that articulates the spaces wherein societies struggle to share common ends, yet exists in a constant state of flux and disrepair from the goals of what had driven this planet from its infancy, into a realization of the potential it may still possess, throughout the cunning of an innocence that assimilates collectives into stratified and incomplete expressions of the whole.

The manner in which we perceive reality to be addressed, as a condition that is still undergoing a transformation of the dispossessed, becomes of the social forms that transcend the concepts that are adaptable to the thrust of human potential, from its core as an existential horizon of a uniform transmission of identifiable resources—still considered palpable to humankind. Those that are immaterial, and those that are now within the grasp of the majority of participants to the technological interstices, where war had once driven the pursuit of happiness to its symbolic collusion with the ideas conforming to world experience, are the same as the stand-alone calculations that donated a natural progression of this life, into its other perspective as the place where existence as a collective would sooner disappear from the universal, than notice that a body-politic had annexed the requisite avowals of a moment in time, where human evolution is becoming more at odds with its own devouring than a calibrated attempt to resolve the disputes that societies and individuals face in consideration of the significations that deliver the message from the position of its Other—and the news is not what we had been hoping for.

Since none of us will be escaping the inevitable circumstances of the logic that possesses a sense of agency over what signifies the very exaltation of the process, whereto a recognition of the valued prospects informing planetary existences are those that confined the spirits to their own undoing as a function of the representation of what had propelled human identity forward—through the birth of its initial genesis as a changeable component of the human psyche—time will become more or less the most significant component to how the Earth will overthrow the same macro realism that birthed modernity, while what gave flight to postmodernism must remain intact, yet undergo an intense restructuration where all is not at stake.

What is at stake however, is the micro universe, where each citizen has a concept of the globe as a space that requires the attentions of what could only be made by a collective potential, embodied by the same regulative passions that had liberated and appealed to the social and political movements that annihilated the injustices that propelled an inequality passed-on between generations—believing that the necessary rights-of-passage had been granted by an altruism driven by its contempt for meaning, and a longing for an avarice that quelled the passions of the spirits, projecting a truth that were more conditioned by a sense of ownership of the realities that were more efficient when life were not a commodity in-itself.

There is a bio-political disunity to the information age, that is only reducible to the form by which it accommodates reason with a decent dosage of despondency for the fruits of social transformation—incurring its debts with society, more than it eventuates a dissolution of the content that condones the absence of its necessary edification of what had never driven its apocalyptic perception—that we are only to destroy ourselves as communities, societies, nation-states, etc., where we destroy our own personhood as though it were a universal power *in toto* that had the potency to crush the naïve realism of an aging population, emerging from a formerly provoked culture that had positioned the world in a mode of abstract necessity.

Though none of us would wish to admit that the existential flaws of the choices that govern subjectivity are the same as those that act as causes to the multitude of disasters facing the planet, should an abstraction from what is already in existence become the form by which choices are delivered to the world at large, we are responsible for what we approach at a distance as something alien to ourselves, and are the cause of what happens to those that enter the contents of the Self, as though it were able to create only insofar as at it would be fully capable of dissolving into a condition of an unmediated and identifiable state of disrepair and irreversible damage.

Societies do it all the time—it's the ones that we find culpable that are these that promulgate the necessity for change, more than an acceptance for the *status quo* as a way toward a more peaceful planetary co-existence.

The present gathers space in the same way as the past had gathered time. For nothing is what it is intended to become, nor is what it might be—without at first seeming contrary to the likelihood that its essential quality, is something other to how it appears in laws that govern perception as though it were more than a distance from the truth of what we are able to fathom reality is.

In confluence with the questions posed by a human need to inquire and investigate an inner meaning to existence, an economy of historical need is now upon us more than it had ever been—the destructive powers of global civilization, have persevered through many impossible battles in order to push through the barriers imposed by societal constraints upon creativity. Yet here in North-America—the continent where everything never seems within wishes and dreams of the dutiful prayers instituted by the protectorate of the controlling bodies that form social infrastructure, away from realization as a universal component to continental thought—what is concrete to human subjectivity is nothing less than a flawed effort to condone the status of those for whom a planetary awakening to what would transcend the scope of collective endeavor, is wallowing in the tales of a class that had first birthed social unrest; into a despair that were only beginning to shatter the hopes for what we might be capable of achieving as a species, worthy of a transmission of ideas more potent than the loss of the identities associated with an emancipatory resistance to populism.

Should we find the concept of ourselves less potent than the content would otherwise have been where contained within a concept itself? Absolutely not. Life is an experience that is imbued with its own natural conditions, that are more prone to need than survival—we assume the positions of those within a willingness to consume art as though it possessed a meaning that were particular to our own self-interest—never looking away from the glimpse into what brings a pleasure best described as something that evokes our psyches with an ownership over the products of our collective imagination.

With this in principle, the subjects that become of the social imagination, that had no bearing upon true artistic merit, are consistently lost to the singularities of those for whom nothing resists the realization of more meaningful acts—yet always succumb to the space where the quest is to become precisely what is desired by the marketplace—and not what would bring real change to the conditions that would determine reality to be more potent than its fictitious predicators in deed have now become. The cultural elites that undermine the symbolism well-suited to abstraction in art—and its predecessors of the underground—would never be the perpetrators of a higher power to universal concepts, than the humanists in filiation with what a symbolic revolution can do for its final resting place in the real world of postmodern artistic achievement.

The world in which we live is all about classification, of those for whom the general thrust of what delivered trust in corporations influencing the minds of their most willing consumers, has now become an absence of belief in a form of knowledge that would be without the compromises of the insular factions that embody artistic privilege; as though its development had not come from the same souls that reproduced the content of humanity with a more vital inner self-realization than the ones now being depicted before the senses of a population—that would rather be bereft its more profound forces of nature, than in a state of wasteful ignorance in order to project a future that were built toward more peaceful new frontiers.

Now that we are well enough into the 21st Century, one must obviate the conditions that exist such as they are, in order to reach a number of certitudes, assertions, and conclusions with respect to the increasing necessity of involvement in the discourse that is to shape the existences that identify Western civilizations, in order to distinguish them from those of our predecessors—those being the societies that forgave individual discourse, in order to promulgate a polemical realism that propelled the substance of free nation-states outside of their identifiable realities as unregulated free-market economies—seeking the exclusions of alien intelligences, and members of groups that had once been demonized and thrown into isolated and unlivable mental conditions.

Society is not a concept that is singular to the planet as something that we know to be universal, yet consistently we concern ourselves with a quest for a universality that will allow us to appropriate the purposes of individuals' intellectual pursuits, such that humanity might pursue a greater good than what is confessedly the will of one stray madman occupying Earth, as the doer of all that is outside of the collective body-politic; and within the ambitions of a species that perceives itself to have evolved beyond a past, where technology were not the instrument of our sense of involvement with the world as a whole—but rather, the barrier between what we might accomplish, and what is for us to admire as the horizon of what we conceive as the totality of those very ambitions that had once belonged to progressive collectives that had been informed by more than mass-enterprise and accessible public opinions alone.

Such as it is, there is no framework in place that exists to accommodate what appears for all intents-and-purposes, to be a global crisis in the wings—we are faced with quite a similar task to the one that had conditioned the 20th Century to become the most radical turning point in history for what had birthed a way-of-life that humanity had seen come to pass, and we must apprehend the projection of what will be required in order to fulfil the natural transition and transformation of what had birthed postmodern naturalism from its early roots seeded by the events of the former past of world history. With this, countries might continue to access what resources we have as a species, before we appeal to the concept that the process which determines the situation that is somewhere down the road—perhaps the thirties and forties of the 21st Century onward—we will face a social transformation that had not been expected, but were there before our very eyes as we were too afraid or distracted by the machines that had enabled us more than the conditions that would be produced by that enablement—only to go unnoticed by the former.

We progress toward an awareness that is cued by a global perception, that seems only afforded a privileged class of self-aggrandizing world figures, that are consistently promoting solutions that in the end, might only be compounding the quarrel that we now have with social involvements that are degenerating public perception into a perspective that had not predicted the outcome that will ultimately come, through a shocking revelation that some us already knew had been coming for five decades or more. What is perceived is not an adequate sense of judgment—where the proposed changes necessarily exist within a logic that differentiates between subjects that possess an ability to pursue change in order to accommodate needs; while not possessing the needs in order to accommodate change. The well-being of the latter had long been what had made them invaluable to humankind, while the former had never been fully realized through a social progress, unable to accommodate a discourse that had fully evolved human nature, beyond a position where it disintegrates into the population's perception that humankind can resolve its problems by initiating an overstimulation of the resources that we have in our possession at the planetary level.

What remains to be seen is whether we are fully able to accommodate a dialectical progression to a philosophy, whereby the transformation that is incumbent upon us *at* the planetary level is within our grasp—or beyond the reach of our understanding. This will neither act as the determination of the former, nor a necessary projection of a logic that will naturalize humanity, beyond its ownership over a humanity that had never proposed to act in favour of a position that has now become of a darkness upon the horizon—but would willfully pursue the projection of an illumination that would otherwise become an impossibility; had we not chosen to acknowledge the situation at hand as dire, and in demand of our attention from an informed degree of inspection that had not been derived by any partisan projections of what will bring history past this natural repetition of the past—easily diagnosable by those that perceived the patterns that have emerged throughout the previous three centuries—and situated them as phenomena representing immanent possibilities.

Introduction

Multi-culturalism had given a democratic identity to a media generality that has become a collectivity of singular thought in a contemporary age. It is resultant of paradigms that are installed in the public consciousness through mass media, and is made possible through the implementation of a system of truth in certain periodicals that abstract events to fasten the mind of its public mind set; in abstraction of a consent-based arrangement with an iconoclastic system of socio-cultural paradigms.

Necessity for the restructuration of a democratic imperative that motions away from sensibility, as a universal condition that is other to the contemporary pedantic classifications that will remove unnecessary items from the list, as such, would deserve immediate relations with a nucleus of value—thereby positing what is contemporaneous of phenomenological beings as authenticated representations—signified through societal transformation.

In the dichotomy between certainties that are unnecessary, yet present of thought in an association of reifications within media systems, and a centrifuge of content based on representations that resolve to none other than what is within an individuated perceptibility, within the discovery of ontological currency in culture, this is now a valuation of the individual in a cultural class—weighted inversely proportional to the occurrence of a labyrinth of representations never reflexive through contemporary paradigms as totalities.

Twentieth century media culture, presented the world with an extremely palatable set of conditions that were technologically biased. These were architectonically erected within certain iconoclasts in television, films, records, periodicals, radio and computer technologies. The epochal directive of these systems of media was the hidden element in this as a political movement founded within a 20th century interest contingently known as the technocrats. These groups operated in much the same way as intelligence works today within espionage, though the element of fascination rests in the notion that their working toward the technological state where human qualities are under secret management, is for the purposes of the improvement of a culture. For the public the instruments are hidden within fabrications that are given to them as entertainment, then they are unconsciously greeted with the "programming" such as it is, that wires them into to a technological assembly of collectivized properties that makes them administrable.

The turn of the century marked a period when the Y2K scare, the notion of computers being wiped of their memories—that turned into a population that was being wiped of theirs—delivered a totality of being to an administration that intended to technologize the population for the purposes of controlling all of the public and private property to their limitless advantage. This gave the culture an opportunity to redefine itself of the same conditions on which it had formerly relied, yet to advance without the former cultural advantages acting as experiences that would slow down its progression toward a more media evolved culture. This also restructured the motivation of media, that it was now more based on a system of representations than it was on the actuality of current events.

What this insisted was that there was a human technology waiting on the horizon, that media super-cultures would evolve to shape the world—with how the world was being "depicted" through the process of media selection. This also delivered to the population an unforeseen power to administrate based on the collectivity of truth itself, that was the public agreement with the events as told within the media; without disputation lest the accusations of being an idiot may arise—inciting public scandal and subsequently destroying the life of any individual. This significant change was that the hierarchies had caused the system to backfire, and were in need of new security measures to reclaim social control. As such the public had to be in direct agreement with them at all times; even if that meant making sure that they were not held as a hidden itinerary to the promotion of a non-existent democracy. The primitive truth was that technological possibility and one were in agreement with the other. An establishment of democratic potentiality through a technologically administrative superstructure that pitted public consensus against the individual was born into the world—the very category that was first responsible for invention in the classified world of itself.

To the futurist, this is an ideal position in which to find a basic political state that contains within its administration any cultural imperative; that thrives on the progress only possible through a collectivization of attributes. It also classifies human beings within this system; that it would be necessary to derive from their economic particulars the internal dynamics of how precisely they fit into the greater picture of a social structure, already based firstly on a paradigm, then a value structure that follows the commensurable administration of viable properties. When this superstructure of modern thought programs the collectives, this is precisely what will be considered to be the representations of the value judgments to the cultural elite; when it identifies from a technological vantage point the human artifice that is induced within a formation that arbitrates qualities based on the representations found within these media systems.

As an associative adjunct to the consideration of what may be considered representation or representations, the technological age advances our notions of what might be known in a phenomenal realm. The same principle that applies to the use of optics in the discovery of cosmic phenomena in near and distant galaxies, is elicited in the discovery of phenomena through an image presented through an optical lens then shown on any screen; most significantly the screens of television sets that once utilized the cathode tube to produce a picture. Identifiable technological improvements in televisions have put many more individuals on what might now be called "bio-satellite".[1] This is a bio-chemical short wave substrate of the corporeal being-in-itself that corresponds neurologically with the ordinance of which socio-cultural forms might be represented through televised media. This is a high security state where any person might be tracked by a corporate entity anywhere on planet Earth via the same satellite mechanisms that run televisions, cell telephones, and other remote devices. More recent technologies link individuals in the same specified manner as was previously noted.[2]

[1] Not to be confused with the artificial satellites of the *Soviet* Space Program, where *biosatellites* put plants and animals in Earth's orbit beginning in 1957—continuing until 1969. Based around a concept where "digital space" is synthetically intertwined with the attributes of substance (*eidos*) of human organisms, and that objects in orbit of the Earth may transmit the latter throughout an extrinsic connection to the former.

[2] This idea emerged in the early 21st Century, after September 11, 2001, where technological developments where within the process of becoming instruments of social and bio-genetic control. Through the work of Hegel and the late Nietzsche *via* Schopenhauer, one may observe the effects of radical industrialization as it succumbs to the technologies that determine human political and economic reality.

Effectively, the technological improvements in media are developmental measures that chase human developments stemming from the mid-fifties with the technocrats. These are the same that have been contained within contemporary media systems in a neo-Platonism of secret media operations.

The nuclear fission on planet Earth greatly influenced the developments of computer technologies as they related to humans of plausible micro-physical inter-relations that will be described as the photon radius of a nuclear object; this means that any system's mass is in direct relation within a radiation manifold as it concurs within the electro-magnetic field of another object of its mass, and the two will thusly be substance related of atomic mass—though through a measurable quotient of decaying electrons that correspond with the photon radius of any given object (as dependant on mass). The experiments with Uranium resulted in what would become the new shape of atomism on planet Earth. This is a state that is administrated of the tools that can separate matter with representations and sub-code, making thought a remnant to what is already being designated by the machine, or a micro-intellect. Any singular directive has for it a piece of equipment in performance of a task, and is presented to the human artifice as what might be delegated of an attribute to an individual; based on possession of the necessary equipment with which to access that particular attribute.

What has been mentioned is the WWII division of computer technology, which makes the necessary suggestion of its contemporaneous relation to the use of the atom bomb in Japan. This instantly makes an historic association that conjoins the notion of nuclear fission with the microchip, if thirty years between those events is collapsed.

This presents the first historic principle in the consideration that technology is chasing the developments of the human intellect.

The notion that a consciousness might be divided into holism further as a result of a nuclear explosion, or that the intention is to discontinue this inter-connectedness, is such that a nation is free to excel in its technological fabrication and manufacturing. It was suggested that the Japanese had computers as early as the nineteen-twenties, and for this reason were subject to such an attack, such that their global position in technology would be greatly reduced. However, this is markedly incorrect, and we now know that splitting the atom is a method of technologizing consciousness. The primary difference in experience is found in nature. Through Spinoza, it is noted that nature responds to the human intellect; sheets of lightning in the sky might be considered separate occurrences from the elements in an individual's contemplation, yet they may transpire with contingent thoughts antecedent to the event. Similarly, we are responsive to the elements in this way that the occurrences leading up to a flash of light are intuitions that are unconsciously derived from nature.

Within a philosophical technology, we discover that the technology does respond to human thought, though in a much different way, and also that this is not as much of a response as it is a replacement of the human properties. For the atomist, the computer template of property dispersal in a collective that is in representation and content a neural net, becomes what will be maintained as the absence of God or Nature, in a system that now provides for its own commercial requirements, yet utilizes those stipulations in the distribution of properties. A new occasion to elicit the "Postmodern Enlightenment" as a movement of contemporary paradigms through current representations, where agreements of a veiled collective positing conditional acceptance become intellectual figures. The possibilities are solvent to either a public in generality, or the commercial output of one corporate body as a subsidiary that delegates its mandate to several smaller administrable bodies. The subterfuge from collectivity is found in a general acceptance of dialectical content, yet also in the agreement of what is commensurate with human value as currency.

The essential difficulty in this circumstance, is the presence of this technology that reinforces the superstructure's collectivity driven mandate. The currency of thought is resolute in its abundance of public generality, and then administrated through this generality into a singular cultural entity that has inherited the wishes of the technocratic regime operating under the specific instructions of a more corporate machinery—responding to the generality with its own programming, then administrating the necessary qualities to those individuals under this rule, and subsequently completing the cycle that proliferates and maintains this technological society.

Where philosophy finds its place then, is within individual certainties. To the philosopher, these are a perversion where they interact with anything that is a sophistry; then reducing contemplation that is autonomous to the point where only the currency present in media might redeem it. Though for this it is revealed that the source of the problem is more readily indicated.

The beginning of a new mode of consciousness that escapes its own perversions, will end in a rebirth of progressive philosophical endeavor. The possibilities of a subject are now recreated within a modern totality of being, as mounted in consciousness in an *a priori* mode. This removes the crippling impact of mass media, and renews the insights that fuel the very abstractions that are paralyzing the individuals vulnerable to this form of facticity. As an antinomy of reason, it is found that in this facticity the system of thought provides what makes pre-cognitions and collective information pools available in abstraction, yet it does nothing to supply the pursuit of thought with the necessary instruments to further a pursuit in Universality—the availability of Absolute Notions, and Pure Reason. It rests with subjective wills and is concerned mainly with a free market environment that disables the individuals that arrive on the scene without an effective platform of dialectical thought. However, this facticity does well in the controls that are mechanical endeavors, where motion through space in its effects is motivated by what is perceptual of conceptually naturalized notions (self-concepts). What it removes from thought are the Absolutes of Genus that are Aristotle's first principles of predication; there is no requirement of abstracting from *Being* what it is in-itself the force that defines a movement through space. This refers to the principle that substance is matter, rather than the consideration that substance is permanent irrespective of the matter of things in-themselves.[3] It is noted that the differentia are never present when in direct relation to a concept that is of its being-in-itself force.

The ideality of this system presupposes a realm of consciousness where all representations and content are held within an infinity that is only perceivable to a subject, and that each action and response that takes place will be contained in a field that is mounted with the use of an artificial reality. This is not the computer generated world as first suggested by the brilliant minds that fashioned it early on in computer animation, nor is it a psychical state that enables visions and conveyances to become of the

[3] Given that Immanuel Kant posits substance as permanent, and the essence of a human soul, it should be noted that in his later work he had begun to realize that things-in-themselves as impossibilities to him, had now become of rights that were instantiated by the presence of the duties that accompanied them.

imagination what they may without interference from commerce directed, coercive superstructures (though in this practice they might be somehow desirable).

This is an extension of a technocratic imperative that moves relations from a culture of reified psychical potentialities, and gives a new Universality to occasions of thought that do not want to encounter any contemporary influence that is detrimental to the progression of a culture.

Firstly, the will as the in-itself of its own phenomenon is now held as a possibility to the subject—that is only perceivable to the subject—unless a conception is posited within this phenomenon as an empty object with which to propose on qualities. The conception within the phenomenon is never understood by any collective whatsoever, and it is a *principium individuationes*[4] of all technological activities(bio-satellite). It follows that this phenomenon will also be the will of an opponent, and it rests on a priori conceptions that the will as magnitude will be held—lest the appropriation of the world is realized through a privation by this opponent. We know that in this phenomenon as empty object, there has already taken place an appropriation, as it is representative of the presence of a collective of properties in exchange that it is being-in-itself found within a magnitude that is the will. This identifies an inherent contradiction in the principle, that the will is independent of all otherness, absent of any a priori analytical judgments, or conceptions that are individuals as things-in-themselves. This also presents the essential problem in the application of an individual pursuit within ontology that is systemized by the technological foundation that manufactures its value requirements—through the appropriation of collective value in the administration of human qualities.

Though the representations found in postmodern media systems identify those qualities within the individuals as subjects, this hierarchical administration is deemed necessary in the maintenance of those cultural identities. However, the cultural identities of the public are made in classifications of generality, followed by implements that are installed within a more paradigmatic thought; that there are no identities also within collectivity that are outside of those of the iconoclasts. These groups that

---

[4] Schopenhauer, *The World as Will and Representation*;. Vol. I and II (*third edition* 1859): *latin*; refers to the concept of a Self that has posited a radical position for what must principle its own individuation, in order to attain an emancipatory self-identification from a Hegelian *Other*.

adopt the efforts of others are geographically containing the greater concerns of those factions that are at the helm of their portion of cultural administration.

It follows that a system of categories would make the necessary classifications of those factions, such that they might be placed within an a priori schemata, and that the furtherance of this would be found in a general classification that was supervenient to the appearance of a collective that would acknowledge this as a presence in culture that stood before the potentiality of an individual in their pursuit of ontology, as a being for possibilities. The endeavor marks an effort that supersedes the confines of any institutionalized truth that is measured by its admission into the stratified class structures, within thought, and is motivated to allow entry within the correct provisions. This insists that a culture's will is more prominent than an individual's, which is logical, yet in practice it is noted that the individual certainty is vanquishing what is held in a collective to present this contingency(the collective) with a content representation at exteriority, that is an abstraction that was present in the conditions of the subject as object before the collective in judgment. What is noted here is that the imagination is playing a lesser role in what is otherwise made possible through elucidation; in being a conceptionist, it is not to be without a quality, but it is to enhance proximal talent with a Universal property that is an Absolute, and places the conditions of consciousness within its *progressus*. [5] There, it is conceivable that abstraction from collectives is less of the matter as things-in-themselves, and more that the resolute wills have become predicates of universals within infinity. This infinity is now being considered as the technological state of awareness that is kept identical to the state that is in the governance of collective properties, held both technologically, and then realized within the individual of their singularity in the conditions as set forward by a legal implement of their cultural classification.

We would now have things in-themselves available through technology, for the purposes of in-itself abstraction of the will, and it would necessitate an administrative endeavor that was formed more of a universal currency, that collective value made its presence within consciousness in the neural net of information—a human commodity that data streams human qualities the same way it sends and receives information. It requires a more

[5] Ibid., p.7; *latin*. A term referring to the progression through space, time and causality.

particular security than one identified by proxy servers that are the administrative outposts working with governments to "firewall" data as they are containing properties.[6]

The security is elevated, yet it fastens a system of governance to universals that make those notions a function of cultural identity as defined by the collectives and technocrats as both influences and sources. It follows that the system is therefore presupposing its own limits with the available conceptions, rather than containing a commerce directive within the technological will, that it is now information as sensation—though not all knowledge is sensation.

We have a phenomenal will that is both sensation, and knowledge as information. The Aristotelian truth is found through the proximity of a computer system in this functionality; yet its magnitude is virtual and within the containments of the digital data stream. This identifies a hidden magnitude that is an instrument to those technocrats certain to the will—where information that is contingent of the text as presence in representation upon the instrumentation, the will that acts in accordance with those as necessary conditions of truth fasten the proximities within the media systems as a governance of what are the representations current with certain attributes; and what are entities that administrate these as currencies in their sourcehood.

For the understanding, this brings a new vehicle of thought into consideration. This is a system based on technology in-itself as a modality.

This is held the same way that governments are held in the management of properties, and must seek its awareness of what are the internal dynamics of a proxy in the particularity of administration of a host of attributes. The inter-connectedness of an information system fails itself when it removes from all possibility the correct information to any individual that is hard-wired to a system terminal.[7] Subsequently this disqualifies any administrative agency of truth from the management of

[6] The idea that the neural network of human sensibility is in synthetic unification with the internet in the information age—we are tied to a logic of what might determine our neurological composition at the outset—in liaison with the relations that we have endeavored to establish as well.

[7] Certainly more the case for early 21st Century persons using technological devices. Since 2001 there have been substantial improvements to the mediating powers demonstrated by the birth of the information age as a full-blown technological revolution.

those properties that have been stripped from the source due to misinformation. This contradiction is necessary to indicate, as our endeavor is to mount from the information terminal an infinity that is only available through a generality that abides with an Absolute of Genus. Otherwise, we would be subject to human wills that were consistently disabling, and simply resolve all such narrow dimensional considerations as were available of everything false or misleading in the attempts to acquire quality within the virtuosity of deception. These are practices in pursuit of a currency, and easily fall into rules that are secured within historicity as actions of the will. In other words, it's more effective of action to simply employ the conventions that get the job done, and decide on models that instill knowledge within any individual, yet are the necessary preparations for a tolerability of the circumstances such as they are.

The significance in an apprehension of a technological infinity is in a hermeneutical abstraction of a sub-code of the collective identity of a neural net in its properties, that are of universal proportions, yet never in Universality. There are then algorithms within information systems that are the instruments of thought acting as artificial ontological objects of experience, and fastening a technological universe that by-passes things-in-themselves at information terminals. The representations of a content and text, operate as though the particulars of a thing-in-itself, and must be classified within a synthetic unity that abstracts from both a proxy terminal of the server as from the actuality of a representation of an image and its content. The infinity of a data stream in information exchange is the inner difference of the repelled in-itself into its object Notion. [8] In this instance, the Notion is the function in abstraction at the computer terminal, and of its collectivity the geographical proportions within the neural net resolving to the actual terminal points in the data stream. The Notion is both the conception of the individual as it is the algorithm in a system, and this is temporalized in perception while flowing contiguously in the stream—contained at its terminal points of the proxy administrations. Here data particulars are administered as code and sub-code to the purposiveness of the user terminal point in the neural net. These become the coordinates

[8] Hegel's concept of the self as a *self-concept*. Though within this text it refers to the object of thought as something unmediated by other beings, just as it does something that is both in synthesis with, and mediated by the machines that one might operate.

within the net of the conditions as they exist in a "currency of action at value". E-commerce then becomes value based in its commercial activity—with a commodity utilized as an actuality of the ontological currency that is in attachment to the product, and critical in the considerations that refer to actual value between two parties. The supply and demand is now in virtual assembly as the weighted scale of properties that have a dynamical relation to substance in a commercial activity, and designate the actual value of a product that is actual in fabrication and value on this contingent basis.

The code identities are the facticity of the system. They work in direct correlation with the software programs in their use, subtly indicating the general interaction between consciousness, and software configuration as administrated. This demonstrates how sub-code dynamics have a similar relation to the human psyche as does nature in its synchronicity, and that through the early administrative and maverick assaults on the use of software as a method of infiltrating a system, the ontological identical of the practice is found contingent to the action of the administrator or hacker.

The objects in a proxy are the value identities of a transaction where the technological synthesis has been made equivocal to the nature of the transaction in the occurrence, where a purchase agreement had taken place. The security value consideration is then modified to the relative currency at collectivity—such as would be administrated contingent of account receivables, in a weighted situational relation of indebtedness.

This is the ordinance of substance at certainty, where the contingency of being is orchestrated through the a priori representations that correspond with perceptual objects. This is what is as known, the totality of being in its contingency, and is in constant negotiation with the aspects of a given situation in its actuality. This actuality is by no means the absolute of circumstance that is understood through the certainty that is within substance present; of this actuality in its concurrent posit as conditions of the respective considerations. This truth is not an abstraction.

The truth that is as it is in substance the Absolute of conditions that are predicable of Genus, is in representational predication as what are conditions in relation. These conditions are the totality of representational objects as objects of association with the *progressus* of conditions—as they are perceived in time as circumstance. This as circumstance is apprehended through consciousness, the totality of being as contingent to the temporality of essence as being for existence.

What are in appearance certainties as objects of their representation are antecedent to natural phenomena, just as they are to the following series of representations as they concur with an occurrence that is within nature as in a technology.[9] An occurrence within nature that is subsequent to a set of certainties that are as negations of the self are concluded in the actuality of an occurrence in nature that is of the elements. The representations are of the certainties as things-in-themselves, that are conditional of the contingency of being—that it is within temporality also the etymological object representation of an occurrence in nature. The certainty representations in an image that has its being as counterpart and in contingency, is as antecedent to the conditions that are natural of being as essence for existence.

The objects as things-in-themselves are contemporaneously certain of these representations as contingencies of being in their actuality. This is a spatial exteriority that is proximal to the counterpart of the representation, and temporalized in synchronicity to the image as representation through "a technological conveyance".

The address proximity of a coordinate that is the spatiality of a condition in a software data event corresponds to the temporality of a perception in a sensuous occasion that is an occurrence in nature. This means that the interaction with a data transmission will act in accordance with sensation of the proxy objects—as they coalesce within the manifold system that is the individual faculty of perceptions from the morphological substrate that are the content representations of a transmission; where the occasion for thought has rendered a property involuntary in the transmission that had transferred the set of systematic conditions toward a proxy absolute that is redesigned—the administrator of the same conditions that are present at the terminal. In the following sections we will explore the dynamics of the systems coordinated by an ontology that

---

[9] A concept where the definition of "natural phenomena" are objects as they exist as components of the human psyche, yet are generated by nature in the monistic sense of Spinoza's *ethics*. The fact that they would also become entwined with a technological substrate, is posited as a function of the signifiers inscribed into the machines—as objects involved with the human activities that they enhance. To suggest that humans are enhanced by technology, however, is not a function of nature so much as the "nature of technology" is to enhance human activities.

is concerned with the notions determining the properties that are both accessible to the technological developments of the previous thirty years or more, and where they stand in relation to form and matter, nature, and the objects of consciousness that are posited by the human mind as it is irrevocably designed through an aestheticization that—wherever we concern ourselves infrequently with the a transformation of the social context where we become positioned as a function to the bio-genesis of what derives human potential forward—action throughout the terrain of our noetic stratification of a logic that is readily diagnosable as induced by the philosophers of the present-past; allowing me to acknowledge the theories of masters that have both recognized and abandoned the conventions of their time in order to perform a most radical attack upon the inheritors of this vast lexicon of substantively unadulterated content with which to become resolute within our own proprietary revolutions. That we should be so fortunate as to thoughtfully conceive of a process wherein we are adept toward an establishment of what is conducive to well-shaped ideas thrusting ahead, the consideration of a moment that had emerged from history would be inviting so as to advocate from our rediscovery of its inventions. May we rest assured that there is to be nothing less of what is expected, but an evocative exploration of the places that had initially brought us to a place that we had deigned to inhabit for a duration of time that had not yet found its conclusion within the aftermath of its consequential evolutionary progression forth.

Chapter 1 Hegel and Schopenhauer's Kant in the information age

As substance is movable of the will—through what are the collectives as magnitudes in their collectivity of the will, adherent to a property in substance that is movable—the relative force of the motion of a property resolves to the proximity of the collective will that it is in relative substance with a subject.

This subject is the selection in agreement of a whole that is as seen the Platonic selection of a group assembly of wills that are weighted against the natural proximity of an attribute.

The neural net as a substance manifold is the technological merge of the human psyche with the technological infinity of an information net, that has end terminals in homes and proxy servers—with the main server independent of these, yet main-framed at the national level for data cross-referencing. These proxies are as previously, the value identities of subjects now in a substance manifold that is a collective of these as relations in a technological magnitude that are the movables in collective assembly of their properties—and as beings-in-themselves are now instruments of the will. This will is the technological will of the necessary conditions of a system of data transmission that operates in conjunction with the human will that "expects" the machinery of technology to function; and with this conception of its functionality as will, operates at the level of perception of both subject and object—which is now both the will of a proxy assembly of properties, and the administrative resource agent that oversees property distribution at proxies and at national information centers. The object will of the proxy assembly is also an algorithm of the collective properties as a magnitude of proxy will, which is an artificial object phenomena that is a technological assembly of human qualities—within a perceptual magnitude that has been pushed into substance from human cognition, in the assembly of cogitations at each independent end terminal in the neural net. The content of a computer terminal constitutes the totality of being in representations of the world, and wills are the constellations of independent wills in proximal magnitudes of a conception—proxy wills of collective properties in administration, and a technological artifice that is an algorithm conditional of the collectivity in the totality of an assembly of beings-in-themselves, which is administrable through the artificial magnitude as an instrument of a technologized consciousness—just as it is an assembly of human properties that are now in an infinite data stream and contingent to the Absolute. That the subjects are predicable now of this technological absolute—in the proxy will of an administration of properties—so is the magnitude available to independent intentionality of the user at an end terminal in the functionality of a computer system. It follows that the representations as on the computer screen are the images-in-representation, that cannot be known as things-in-themselves, but that the being-in-itself of these representations is known in substance again through the proxy configuration that is the will of a collective administration.

That the world is contained within these as representations, the algorithm that is the assembly of information into a contingency of being of a conditional data Absolute—the relational object phenomena in consciousness that has the phenomenal quality of an artificial magnitude of a software algorithm—will be representative of a being-in-itself within substance of intentionality in a conveyance, and also the proxy collectivity of an administration in pursuit of a quality that is absorbed into the Data Absolute, that it is also the technological enhancement of a human artifice in substance—without the direct manipulation of an image or text, the ontico-ontological[10] technological artifice is "offering" the Data Absolute[11] to being-in-itself; just as it is absorbing these properties from a collective will. Moreover, it develops the sense of distribution of a properties based on the predication of substance as it works in through collective will to develop its purposiveness. As in its origin, it is within

[10] Heideggerian term that refers to the factual existence of the physical Self (ontic), and the mind-substance of the object of consciousness and its representations of and to other selves through thought and *being* (ontological).

[11] This idea is based upon the concept that mathematical possibilities that are infinite to humanity, are more absolute in the technological sense—as encrypted data cannot necessarily be changed, unless it is interrupted through human intervention. In essence, the Earth rotates at approximately the same rate as the information identified as its rate of rotation may inform us.

Universality, the infinity of the Absolute where its human predication is a temporalization of intentionality, and the distribution of wills in an administration. The predication of beings-in-themselves through this as a magnitude is a corruption of the Data Absolute where it falls from the infinity of Universality into what circulates within a collective and is then within a proxy assembly.

What is conditional at exteriority, is causal of technological representations as correlates in the assembly of interior conditions. This is antecedent to a maxim of commonality that is its general rule of administrative assembly in a representational void that awaits the instructions of a technological artifice. This state is a mode of consciousness that promulgates the techno-cultural representations *a priori*, that elicit the conditions as available from the representation—from which they are contained within as general qualities responsive to those conditions. This is a representational form of administration that encumbers the subject with the necessary technological conditions to implement the system as required, while assembling within the human artifice the sensibility requisite of the ontological ordinance requisite in human pursuits. Substance is held from the technological representation as it mounts within consciousness the possibility of another sensibility, that is in ordinance with the existing conditions as provided in the representation. The form of knowledge is the techno-substrate[12] of the interconnectedness of a manifold information template that is common in its end terminals, and individuated of its purposiveness:— the *negationes* as proxy antecedent to the information as conditions is the administrative assembly as the void of consciousness in its administrative state. The attainment of any information—is the general condition of a particular state of conditions that mount the morphological substrate of those conditions within consciousness as the template to considerations within that department of knowledge. Sensation is the phenomena of a proxy will that is not within this system as substrate, and yet is within the commonality of the general substrate of the information net that is consciousness.

The Universal substrate of the collective that is a general commonality of information possibilities has as its phenomena the will of otherness, that

---

[12] As an idea, where technology and humanity are interconnected, the substratum of each may be understood through an algorithm that is a result of a possible synthesis of the two.

is subject in conception of their totality of being, which is from this now relational to the administrative void of consciousness of this commonality and without its inherent purposiveness. This is conditional to the presence of images-in-representation that are the re-constitution of a composite self that has been technologized from the end terminal as such. The user terminal purposiveness is conditional of the information in request as proxy conditions of an informational request where those properties are the morphological configurations of a system of information.

Phenomena in the psychical form of knowledge—that is contiguous to the information proxy—is its proxy contingency of being in presence of the subject as its object Notion. Contemporaneous with the information in the assembly of objects is a manifold that represents the proximal Notion to the subject of the request for information—that is granted of this as a directive of the end terminal assembly. It follows then that the subject must acknowledge a priori the host conditions at proxies and at the proximal terminals where the conditions of information as supplied are contingent to the Object Notion, as supplied of the proxy terminal that has sent this contemporaneously with the data request. This Object Notion is the unconditioned of the condition—as found within the data request that it mounts within consciousness, the implements necessary of the disclosure that is found in conclusion of the *progressus* from truth in the facticity that is in accordance with the conditional assembly of situational objects, that are in accordance with the truth of this as a pursuit in a techno-ontological disclosure of the associative information assembly as a synthetic unity of facticity that is edified within truth. The manifold object relations resultant of a data request are in accordance with the data absolute of a conditional truth that has in disclosure the related quality of a subject, within the initial condition of an information request toward the unconditioned of a data absolute. The conditions as in presence—that are in techno-representation[13]—are now in contrariness of the object Notion as unconditioned; that they are *in abstracto* of proximal attributes that are relational of the information as in disclosure to the subject. It follows that

[13] Ibid., p. 16. The essential idea that technology has for its representation in "digital space", accounts for the network of projected noumenal beings more in filiation with the developmental technologies of the two first decades of the 21st Century. However, the conceptual form by which representations are stratified to artificial intelligence, suggests that representational being is evolving with technology synthetically.

these conditions must be held a priori to the proxy objects as a substrate to the perusal of information in representation that they are of things-in-themselves a conditional assembly of proxies that mount the necessary conditions of an information document without certainty in presence. The techno-representations are the proxy end terminal conditions of beings-in-themselves, yet these as objects are never known from there representations in-themselves,—yet the form of an Object Notion is the phenomena as content to the beings-in-themselves that are known from conceptions of the will.[14]

Conditional representations as content in an action that are known actual of exterior contingencies of being

This is the human state where a content representation is in appearance antecedent to the actuality which is then considered contingent of being—where the effect from Causality is never actual, yet in representation contained as the substance that reproduces the contingency in thought; making known the conditions that are in thought of an object, such that the conditions as effects are realized in reciprocity to the representation. What posits these same considerations, are the effects as conditions within Causality—then always the antecedent affirmations to the affirmation of a negation that is the exterior negation of an interior affirmative posit; that makes necessary an exterior negation in effect of a causal affirmation. This designates the representational in-itself a priori to the posit of an affirmation of conditions as effects that are antecedent to the exterior reciprocity that is concurrent to the posit as apodictic truth.

The principle of negation is the negation of a negation, that the posit is causal to an affirmation of a set of conditions; then what is in derivation as influence is the antecedent to a subject reciprocity as negation, then the

[14] this considers the concept that subjectivity—while intentional toward an object (*Husserl's cogito*), such as a technological device may not be known as a being-in-itself. The encounter with Hegel's self-concept is realized more through a representational, subjective will—conclusively more to the appearances that stand awaiting their symbolization during ontological reflection; nested in image-signs from Nietzsche to Freud.

exterior negation is the response to an influence that is the object of reciprocity.

The contingent being as conditional truth in an antinomy of reason

Being in representation is apprehended of the conditions in relation, and is its content from the standpoint of a hermeneutical etymology—that posits these conditions as content a priori. This is its determinateness in principle, and differs from object certainty from what is conditional of truth at an abstraction of collectivity that is its genera, as is its possibility in perception of the subject. The content of a will within collectivity is a set of possibilities, in a generality that is of its collectivity the Genus of the conditions at possibility; this articulates the individual life force of its will within Genus. The certainty as will posits itself within substance that is as truth the collective possibilities—within the perceptual object of its magnitude.

The determinateness within substance is truth of the conditions in relation to a subject, both within the contingency of being of possibility; just as they are the necessary conditions in relation of an actuality that is certain of truth and known a priori. The necessary appearance of a content that is a posit of set conditions outside of a certainty and known a priori, is the truth of the conditions that exist as possibility for a subject—indicating the conditions in relation in a subject-object intercourse. The perceived content is of truth, as it is necessarily true of the conditions in relation to the possibilities that are perceivable to the subject—in a generality that is in a unified collective of equanimity with instrumental magnitudes that are in representation, the objects of experience. Rather, the manifold relation of several contingencies of being in temporal relation as otherness known as beings-in-themselves—that collectively possess an individual contingency of being that is assembled and mounted within consciousness; in an amalgam of the conditions of beings-in-themselves in collectives at an ideality. This differs from the generality of publicness, as it has a realist aesthetic that disassembles the uniformity of a conditional truth—that is the objects in relation and of their contingencies of being realized in a collective of relativist possibilities. The futurist ploy to claim this collective possibility in a certainty is dismissed—on the grounds that it is in relation with a conditional truth while maintaining the necessary truth of the content in representation of the object as opponent—in an interplay that discloses the necessary conditions of truth without a certainty. This has for its object a magnitude that is an image-representation, and has of its content a phenomenon that is an empty object—in-itself substance—then acting as its own Notion for the possibility that is before the collective will of certainty; which is in truth the possibility of an object as it meets the conditions of what is held in perception of a subject. This is the collective of possibilities in contingency of a conditional possibility based on the situation. The Notion that is encumbered with an empty object is its will that is the in-itself of a perceptual inclusion of possibility—the phenomenon of what is in perception the exteriority of an inner conditional truth. The exteriority of an object as being-for-itself and in presence that is its physical appearance, is the image-in-representation for an object that its will is the phenomenon of an empty object of its Notion within thought—that is the possibility of an object that has a subject in view that is willful of possibility and general to the conditions of the subject; of truth in relation to the subject of a reflective in-itself that discloses the truth possibility to an object in actuality of appearance—that this is the contingent possibility of a being-for-itself that it is in perception of a subject and of collectivity a conditional (relativist) truth to a subject. The representations of the conditional truth of an object in relation are as judgments antecedent to the *a posteriori* judgments of the subject as certainties, and of truth are known to the subject a priori both in the contingency of being, and as actualities that are conditional of truth for the subject; the action of the contingent being as object. A certainty that is in representation at conditional truth of a subject is for an object a synthetic judgment.[15]

An image-in-representation as being-for-itself as will is not known in-itself, that the Notion is a contingency of being at potentiality; that is the conditional truth of the subject in knowing the object of this contingency

[15] Kant, *Critique of Pure Reason* (1781). While building upon the idea that judgments yield objects before *(a priori)* or after (*a posteriori*) experience, the concept that continues to be perplexing is that the thing-in-itself (contingency) remains in its effect.

of its conditions a priori. The being as matter-in-itself can only be known in physical appearance with a rectilinear projection that is with an a priori conception, just as the being-in-itself of a possibility that is in image-representation of will from an object is the conditional truth of a being-for-itself, that can not be known in-itself of its object, yet can be known as matter-in-itself of its physical contingency of being with a general conception. The image as object is never known in-itself, yet is certain of will as a being-for-itself, not of truth—that it is not known as matter-in-itself of the contingency of being rule, that is a conditional truth in a subject-object inter-play that is both the a priori conditional truth of a contingent being; within the principle of a conditional truth of being that the representation is within a circumstance, which is known in-itself contemporaneously of the a priori conditional truth from possibility in appearance, and the will in image representation that is within sufficient reason the certainty of an object that can only be known as a being-in-itself with a different conception than what is presented as content in an a priori conditional truth.[16] The immutability of an action that is of truth is positioned in contrast to the certainty—justifiable of reason that is being-for-itself, not yet known in-itself of the will that is in image the spatial abstraction of a set of conditions contingent within the truth of a subject in a potentiality; though in conception of its conditions as possibility, the being-in-itself of an object as subject from image representation. That is the being-in-itself of "the will as the in-itself of its own phenomenon";—the phenomenal will in-itself as a contingency of being to the truth of an image representation, and truth of a contingency of being to the will in an image representation.

Being-in-itself is its Object Notion, and contingent to the truth of an a priori conditional truth that is in appearance of the will and of its content, a being-for-itself. The Notion is the phenomenon of the will of its object, that is an a priori conception to the in-itself that repels into the Object Notion. Both the in-itself of the subject and of the object are within this object as Notion, that is without a representational differential in the contingency of being. The image representation is the situational

[16] Of an idea formed by Schopenhauer, given that a Kantian conception is particular to the transcendental aesthetic. Though from here, I would wish to position utility where the symbolization of the image-object is independent of material form, while the objects within the representation are logical signs to which subjectivity finds an epistemological realism.

determinateness of an object, that is of its content at the Notion with a condition of being that identifies a conditional truth as a possibility within a circumstance. These wills are of their determinateness beings-in-themselves as noumena and responsive to pure negation of the phenomenal will.

Dynamical Representations in Nature

That occurrences in nature are dynamically contemporaneous with a relational object, an a priori judgment is contemporaneous with the "instruments" of an occurrence in nature; that *a posteriori* experience is antecedent to the cause. Magnitudes of nature (thunder, wind, rain) will be identified as the phenomena of an actual spatial magnitude that is the community relation of an inverted ratio of space that is posited within the spatial elements as a pure conception of the understanding. This is realized empirically—where the forms of things are understood as the content of a space, and where substance is the abstraction of space that is matter understood as time. Of this as a presence within Genus—natural magnitudes as phenomena—the form of knowledge is truth as a synthetic unity of the understanding. As a principle of causality, this presents the determination of a causality (that is its conception of a necessity), that posits phenomena from a synthetic unity. These are all generated by the mind a priori and the empirical intuitions that are phenomenal objects.

That a contemporaneous representation of certainty still may be known in reflection of a representational object, things are yet not known in themselves, that this certainty is conditional with what is a natural reflection of an object of the representational self; such as the physical reflection of the body from a mirror. This same reflection that is conditional of a representational self-cognition is also available within the elements of nature proper, such as would be reminiscent of the tale of Narcissus. A non-contemporaneous representation of a representational object in reflection that presents in an object the content of a being-in-itself as object of a phenomenon, are merely the contingent perceptions of other objects that hold in thought the conditional apprehensions of the self as subject, in conception that is known from this temporality within an infinite reflection; where the reflective image-in-representation of the self as object is attuned to the perceptions of a infinite series of judgments that meet with the conditions of the current representation when perceived in a *regressus*. [17] In actuality, the mirrored reflection of the physical being-in-itself as self is the conception of the object that is using the understanding contemporaneous with an image-representation, thereby in regressus of the subject; that the subject is unable to know the mirrored self in-itself—yet that the image is infinitely projected, it is only known in what is repelled from the in-itself into substance as content in the form of phenomena. This is the reflected in-itself that has for it the quality of judgment of otherness, that is in conception of the image-in-representation, contemporaneous with its certainty and with its conditional truth that is the necessary condition of judgment. That is also from the unconditioned, from the image-in-representation that was contingent to the understanding.

The world is finite in representation, yet it is in infinite regressus, acknowledging what was already a thing-in-itself, that the unconditioned of all possibility had expressed itself to the conditions of an image-in-representation, as the superscope of a collective that presented the particulars of a subject-object relation in representation.[18] The form of an image-in-representation is the image of a situational object of its conditions as content, and cannot be known of its phenomena as a being-in-itself. Though from the contemporaneous magnitude, is known in-itself through the conditions as content in a synthetic proposition as truth of its magnitude; that is yet now only the possibility for the subject-object in consideration. A situational object that is its representation is found within the conditions of the image-in-representation. Representations are of the *conditioned*, and present the condition or conditions of a situational

---

[17] Ibid., p.7. A term utilized by Schopenhauer referring to a return of a representation that is an image, phenomenon, or noumenon that has been abstracted from the Kantian unconditioned—thereby resulting in a concept of the other as an identifiable being to consciousness.

[18] The notion that image-signs become visible to communities or collectives, and become particular to the former and the latter respectively is here defined as the disclosure of mental representations to the former as a function of something such as Plato's cave as in Book Seven of the *Republic*. That is would be actual to the former would be reason for its identification as such.

object from possibility of its content and its form as phenomena in an image.

Sensation is the in-itself of an object from the will that has for it as its phenomenon the image-in-representation—when for this image the content of phenomena is the form of sensation as truth in the contingency of being. That we are affected by objects through the form of knowledge that is sensation, by the faculty of representation alone, we do not experience sensation with images-in-representation as a unified form of knowledge that is truth without the awareness of a conditional truth in the contingency of being. It follows that in consideration of infinite representations, the image-in-representations would present the quality of a contingent being that was in possibility of a contemporaneous relational dynamic; yet that the knowledge of sensation would present the world as matter, of some configuration of relations before the collectivity of an arena of ontological representations as a contemporary truth of the collective. That this collective is representational of the relational contingency of being, is the foundation for the postulate that is conditional truth. That these are contemporaneous with sensation as being-in-itself with images-in-representation, remains the next mystery to unravel.

Now matter-in-itself [19] is conditional in conception of the unconditioned, which is the ideation of a collectivity, that is of a universal substratum that is of a teleological end; for the Object Notion it offers no synthesis in proposition that posits a notion beyond this collective as a terminal point of thought. Though from this human teleological end emerges forward the morphology of a spatial magnitude, that presents from conceptions the world in-itself as sensation, with contemporaneous images-in-representation. It is proposed that this would be due to an infinite reflection in accordance with the images. While finite in reflection of its images-in-representation, it also relates to a representational object that is from this in infinite *regressus* of the subject from the unconditioned. This unconditioned is the conditionality of a being-in-itself, as it relates to the Notion of a finitude of the substrate of matter-in-itself of its content. That form of itself represents the content of a space, matter-in-itself is reserved for the form of knowledge that is sensation—as the magnitude of beings-in-themselves. That this is in conception, the

[19] The concept that physical matter, at the atomic level—possessing qualities becoming identifiable as substances—may be known in-themselves as objects of thought. Ibid., p. 6., p. 21.

form of space as matter-in-magnitude, the substrate is notioned of its universality that the situational object is now an unconditioned contemporaneous reflection that is conditioned of its own reflection.

This being-in-itself of its substrate is the template of causality, from which a natural occurrence is predicable of Genus that interacts with the course of events in Nature; that is predicable of these that Nature herself is also found in morphological representations antecedent to the cause.

When it is the case that existence would precede essence, it is that a conception of the self is necessary in the preservation of any essence that is contiguous with existence, in contemporaneous action of the essence in proximity of an individual. What is here in presence is the genera as principle in the conditions of relational being, that posits the self a priori of its own Object Notion in representation, and from conceptions of the unconditioned gives images-in-representation. It follows that a discussion on the amphiboly of tech-genera[20] as relational beings, and existence as administrative essence would commensurate with the nouveau of our cultural assembly in an analytic.

What is referred to as tech-genera, are the contemporary proxy relations that confer with an information system. That the information itself is in representation of its document morphology *per se*, it is that the proxy relations are found in an immediate relation of their conditions as being-in-itself within a magnitude; that is the sensation of a will with what is antithetical to an epistemology that is contiguous with the document information. That these a priori relations are in relation to the subject of another purposiveness that is contained within the document information, as content, the phenomenal will resolves to the collectivity of a relational tech-genera in conjunction with the contemporaneity of a conditional acquisition of data, that is selective of that very process where distributes the associated attributes. Everything that is relational of the concomitant dynamical associations, within a collectivity of individual purposiveness, in pursuit of the information in its initial documentation and its related morphological structures that are in relational association of corporate contingents, constitutes the primary schematization of what is structural of existence as a first principle of being as tech-genera.

---

[20] A concept that materializes the genesis of what had occurred upon the 21st Century's horizon—a generation that were in the process of merging with the content and the forms of technology itself—as though it had become particular to Aristotle's *Metaphysics* and *Nicomachean Ethics*.

That this is in principle of a genera, it is the attributes as they are held contiguous with the proxies of relational objects in their collective purposiveness as they are assigned to a generality of a resource of attributes. These are conditional with the content of information to the subject *a priori.* From this it is that the proxy maintenance of a host of human qualities are transferred into their collective purposiveness, then of the information as morphology that they are predicated of in part by the individual of the information as purposiveness—where the information properties are supplanted to the proximal human artifice and put in relation to the essential qualities of the subject. That this proximal essence is now interacted with, the qualities that are of their nature known a priori in their proxy relational collectivity act as morphic properties to the subject, then sometimes replace the subject of its Object Notion—in conjunction with the collective purposiveness of its tech-genera. That this is as principle known a priori, it is that the essence of qualities that are in motion with the data request of a purposiveness are in the attainment of information. The information is introduced into the property configuration of an individual, that must then predicate of those host properties, with the containments of which they are the essence as qualities of initial purposiveness in relation to the morphological properties of the collective purposiveness; contained within the conditions that are inherent of the system of information, and its dynamical association of properties in the contemporaneous relations of being that are conditionally associated with the structure of conditions in a data request. This is its profession.

The data request of a tech-genera assembly—in the preservation of a data resource as principle—magnifies the proxy relations of existence as tech-genera where the properties are made representational by the information of documents that are in contemporaneous representation of technology, and of representational conditions the associated contingents. In association, these collectives of relational interest are known a priori, within a morphology that is represented in the information as the representational form of knowledge; then as sensation phenomena in the form of the will. This will is a component of the assembly in property maintenance that administrates the qualities as found in the collectivity of purposiveness of the tech-genera. It is then that a generality of contemporaneous information availability in an a priori relational morphology works in conjunction with the data cross-referencing of a government agency that acts in accordance with the currency of a proxy authority. This is within a general information maintenance that is attributable to the administrative contingents that are working in commiseration with an a priori necessity of data acquisition; resolving to a proximal vituperation as a primary existent posterior to the request for datum.[21] This is contradictory to the value management that is inherent of the initial coalition of properties introduced of a data request, that are then merged with the provincial and federal administrative assemblies in the preservation of what is the necessary protocol of property maintenance of their natural geography. From this in conception, is what contains those very properties in their particularity in representation; which hosts the qualities of the terminal points, in relation to a national assembly of qualities contingent with the aspects in particularity that are necessary in the acquisition of information. Then within a configuration of administrative enforcement, as the conceptual morphology of a host property contingent is adapted to the essence of a proximal subject, this is within existence contiguous to the interchange of properties in a data-information acquisition. The totality of being is submerged in a situational interplay with the a priori relational contingencies of proxy purposiveness, with the *a posteriori* governmental administrative authorities that also act as influence in accordance with the subjects that are in maintenance of those properties commiserate with the profession. This invariably does supersede essence as an existence, yet it yields an *a priori* principle of *Cogito* supervenience. This introduces into causality the antecedent to what is principled to genera, the movability of properties that are then introduced into a collectivity of relational attributes within a proxy, and its posterior analytic that is administrative to the representation of authorities that are present in the containments of these qualities as they are resolute to the contemporary requirements of a nation-state. This, in its resolution, is the *reductio ad absurdum* of the subject, where presuppositions are not induced into the data authority, and are principled of the relational resource of qualities, as contained within situational assemblies of resource attributes as they combine with proximal attributes in their contingency; that they have they been superseded by a morphology of information that has delivered associated qualities *a priori*. This subsequent maintenance and recovery becomes subjectivity in-itself—

[21] There has as the world knows all-too-well been an exposé upon this phenomenon (WikiLeaks (founded in Iceland 2006)), founder Assange, Julian ; and (Cambridge Analytica 2018 (the *Facebook* scandal)).

where these qualities had entered a sphere in relation to the "now", as contingency to a proximity of relational attributes contained within the morphic schemata of the information as host quality. In this respect, the morphology of information as existence that precedes essence, is in perpetual conflict with an essence that has a priori access to information resource properties of those *affiliated* administrative assemblies. From the cultural standpoint, this mounts an essential a priori configuration of informational consciousness, directly in relation to the administrative purposiveness of collectives in contingency of conditional property acquisition. The information remains in its representation, the end terminal of data, in the necessary conditions of being in association with the conditions contained within the information, and the contingency of *being* becomes the truth of a subject in relation to the information, and *ipso facto* to the actuality of a subject. This as a maintenance, denies the principle of tech-genera as a principle of the reproduction of a species, contemporaneous with thought information; yet reveals the inherent merge that occurs within the contingencies of being, from the representations as in presence within nature antecedent to cause, as an essential dichotomy in the relational being that is induced of the motion of qualities into a proxy resource, that supersedes the proximal qualities of a subject. The representations as authorities from technology in a morphology of attribute resources, are directly associated with previously mentioned information systems in what will be called A Natural Law of Universal Information. [22]

This is a rule that secures the essential quality of information—in all systems as an absolute of data that principles content to the particularity of the necessary morphic systems as edified of the concurrent cultural requirement; and necessitates the protocol of these requirements of their terminality in the preservation of the proximity of the status requirement in an information system. In its relational quality, the information that is generalized in all systems finds the individual purposiveness in resource as a contingency of being. This contingency of being is maintained of otherness within a system of being that is blocked, that from its existence in actuality, it is in conflict with an object that operates under similar

[22] This is resolutely becoming more possible due to technological advances moving toward the coming centuries—that nature and information would be interlinked as causal not only to an outcome for humanity, but also the principles that govern natural law (the extensions and the boundaries of science).

conditions, that are of those implements in conveyance that is contained within the information itself. It follows that as *Beings* we are now standing in relation to the information itself, as the primary form of communication that is in comparison to a phenomena of its content; the nature of an information system, of its presence in proximity as the actuality of all related phenomenal encounters that are present of the information.

In all forms of media are found the following classifications of information: content relational facticity, morphological representations, and images and renderings. Inherent of all representations within media systems is their phenomena, that is a relational magnitude that mounts a contingency of collective being in the universality of information as an informational substrate in direct correlation with the substrate of Nature as it is within a consciousness relational. For instance, if we hear about hurricane Eddy on the 6 O' Clock news, read it in the paper, receive updates on the internet, or talk about it over the telephone, etc., we are all participating in the information substrate of causality that may be the potentiality of the destructive force of hurricane Eddy. That Eddy might also be in arrears of some of his personal debts, also demonstrates the relational quality between humans and nature; based on the indebtedness of society toward Eddy and vice versa, where concerns the magnitude of force present of its relative essence in the movement of force from Nature of this destructive magnitude. That this informational coalescence, that refers to the collective cogitation of this hurricane as a magnitude of Nature, is contained in its contingency of the actuality of being in the force of Nature. This is the causality of an information system, as principle to the consciousness of the awareness principle; that what is natural to awareness is the occurrence of phenomena. That we have awareness in our contingencies of information systems—then that these are within universal information systems in forms of media that address occurrences in nature—is causal of the awareness of a phenomenal information system from a technological contingency of being. From here there is a confusion between the actuality in truth, and the contingency of truth that comes as no great surprise. The morphological representations refer to the inherence of structures within a philology of media systems, that edify super-structures of cultural authority—with a media itinerary that mounts the factual contents of a media system as an a priori form of conditional knowledge. This acts as a causal system, in the awareness of an occurrence as it relates to media configurations. The practice of abstraction for the proliferation of media systems, is causal to the conditions that set the containments of things-in-themselves; as these are composite relational truths that are not necessarily true of facticity—for the basic configuration of a causal media system to implement the conditions of societal contingents, is in agreement with the currency of events. Here the truth is a proximal instrument of the information superstructures that present quality management as an existential mandate, in place of the absolutes of the currency of information. In this sense, the morphology of language is an informational substrate to the intuitional substrate within Nature; that its interactive teleology of Nature as Notion is contiguous with an existential informational system that precedes the essence of a subject and ultimately of a population.

The idea as contained within Nature, is in advance of its Notion the motion of an awareness toward an absolute that is the Notion as contained within a thing-in-itself. A tree is in its Notion only relational to us such that it is a representation of an object—that it is in its form within the idea of what is an existent such as is presented in that configuration of its essence. Its life force is relational to the elements of Nature, yet is in perception relational to a subject as an idea. With the awareness of this as an idea it is that the subject apprehends the self through this idea, that the self is representational to the rest of nature in this simplicity of its essence *as* idea. That this is also informational to the subject—as without the presence of this idea there would be no consideration that accompanied it—is its Notion within the absolute of a Notionality[23] that is the absolute of the presence of ideas within Nature. That these precede the existence of all animal life, is the basis of understanding what existence precedes, in the essence of Nature from its first principle of the genus of a species. For the order of Nature to precede this principle of Genus structures the absolute of movability in the ideation of any information system that supersedes the Genus principle of the human species.

Throughout the ages it has been that technology chases humanity. Humankind fashions the source of knowledge and the tools that are required to evolve manufactures of our being toward a more sophisticated way of life.

---

[23] Hegel—the idea that a self might be constituted in-itself by its own ontological objectification as the very being of its own conception.

The Awareness Principle of a Natural Occurrence

I This is a metaphysic within causality that is both an occurrence in Nature and a "natural" occurrence.

II A natural occurrence is also an occurrence in Nature.

A- What is natural to phenomena is both the nature of phenomena, as what is the phenomena of an occurrence in Nature.

B- Awareness is the nature of an occurrence.

(i) What is natural to awareness is the occurrence of phenomena.

(ii) An occurrence is the phenomena of an awareness.

C- The content of a phenomena in nature is the awareness of an occurrence.

The phenomena of content is the occurrence of its awareness.

(ii)The occurrence of phenomena is the awareness of its content.

<u>Genus</u>

I An occurrence in Nature has both its natural phenomena and its natural effects “expressed” in the perception of the individual.

II A natural occurrence is causality of an occurrence in Genus that is an occurrence in one of the elements of nature the end point of causality.

(2)

(i) Space as occupied by an occurrence of Nature is the phenomena of a natural occurrence.

(ii) A natural occurrence is the phenomena of an occurrence in space.

(3)

A thought as an occurrence is both its natural phenomenon and natural occurrence, that thought is the nature of phenomena in an occasion of Nature, i.e., I think of a traffic light changing and the wind blows a telephone poll over.

An occurrence in Nature can never be thought away antecedent to the cause.

(i) The content of a consideration subsequent to and consistent with the necessary conditions of a manifold of relations can be antecedent to an occurrence in Nature.

(ii) The mechanical conditions of a natural occurrence in space are perceptually antecedent to a subsequent occurrence in Nature as it is thought; and is contemporaneous with the conclusive series of a set of conditions at exteriority. (this is also a magnitude within nature as the phenomena of the will).

Nature can be known in-itself as both the will of its phenomena and the phenomena of the (human) will.

The Genus Principle of Sensuous Abstraction

I

(i) Sensuous properties are known within objects of experience *a priori*.

(ii) Objects of experience are manifold properties in contrariness.

(iii) Objects are posited *a posteriori* to the apprehension of an object.

II

General Rule

A physionomy of connected properties is known cogitatively before the substratum of substance.

(i) In the abstraction of sensuous properties from the substratum of substance, the content of its Notion is posited of its Notion *a priori*; it follows that the property of the substratum is not connected as a correlate of objects and instruments of experience by the faculty of cognition.

(ii) A sensuous property is pushed into substance with a "conception object"; found as an object of experience then abstracted as an object in-itself of the sensuous property.

Manifold Certainty Negation

A rule is formed of manifold properties that is posited *a priori* to cancel certainty in assertion.

(i) Each manifold in its modality composes the system which abstracts of each item in conception.(an a priori synthetic unity that holds contraries of the in-itself to action as differentia).

This proposes an a priori conception of the in-itself for the maintenance of a property in its proximity, then discloses another quality as differentia within itself, that it is not a connected attribute entirely susceptible to the will.

Each function of the being-in-itself at collectivity is the magnitude of substance and of the conception in its magnitude the collective matter of a certainty that is in its collectivity, a truth.

The necessary modes of conveyance in a thought that is contemporaneously understood are as follows:

(i) object in representation

(ii) object of experience as phenomenon

(iii) object will, the in-itself of its own phenomenon (as magnitude)

(iv) truth in proximity of the in-itself as a collective magnitude

(v) certainty within substance that is the content of an a priori conception(of an attribute).

(vi) image as representation of a situational object

Artificial Representational Systems

The technological conditions as found in an artificial system that has of its technological properties a set of possibilities, such as are put to use from its multi-functionality, has as its contingency of being the content as representation in consciousness that is an epistemological description of the technological occurrence concerning the artifice of a technology, i.e., you are being ripped off ... This is *state of occasion* within the technological possibilities and is realized as another contingency of being that indicates a possibility at exteriority.

I

The world is an unconditioned whole, that it exists *in-itself* as a magnitude. In a series of causes and effects it exists through the *regressus* of the representations of them. This presupposes the unconditioned as infinity, though containing definite conclusions as determinateness in a series of conditions that exist independently of the representations. It follows that the representations exist independently of the world as will. These are infinite in their determinateness of unconditioned conceptions in forms of knowledge. The "effect" from cause as will is the determinateness in a series of conditions conclusive and finite. Representations without effect from causation are infinite and of the unconditioned though in determinateness of a will within a series of conditions.

II

The world exists contingently to a mental picture or representation of a subject upon transcendent horizons of thought.

i) An infinity of conditions as known *a priori* must be finite in representation of conditions that can be known with conceptions.

ii) The infinite series cannot presuppose infinite *regressus*, as regressus is also unconditioned of a condition that is its conception; and from causation the conception of infinity.

iii) An infinite series moves in *progressus* from the unconditioned that posits causal conceptions—bound within a series of conditions that meet their conclusion as determinations that are finite to the forms of knowledge.

Relative Space

This is the position of an object or point in space in reference to another point in space, and how force describes its mass as magnitude where force is light in the form of radiation that reveals its point in space, that time is matter; that matter is predicable of radiation as form-radiation is not predicable of matter.

Quantum Expressions through matter and time

Part I- Form and Matter

(i) the velocity of mass from force through relative space articulates the form of time as matter.

ii) form is separable from matter as matter is predicable of form, yet form is not predicable of matter and exists as relative space.

(iii) time is matter.

Part II- Form in Historicity

(i) Form is independent of the considerations of matter.

(ii) "Magnitudes of Historicity" are in consideration of form and of matter as time.

(iii) Force through matter in relative space as magnitudes of time, is the magnitude of force in time and correspondent with matter.

(iv) The magnitudes of historicity are things-in-themselves as forms and in time as matter and the conditions of matter are predicable of form.

(v) The magnitudes of historicity in the force of magnitude through relative space in form of magnitude, posits *a priori* in the (intuitions) of immediate space—correspondent with the super-posed quantum states of force through relative space, into the form as force in magnitude that time is matter.

Part III- Matter and Force

(i) Mass is relative to velocity from force in the consideration of matter through space.

(ii) That this consideration is stretched through light time, between two points, A-B, it is put into consideration that the relative velocity as mass is the principle of matter as time; that only through force as velocity through light space (the distance between two points) is the consideration that mass is relative.

(iii) Only in this consideration is matter known in time as form.

(iv) Form is known in time without velocity.

(i) Form is separate from velocity.

(ii) The distance of light travelled is force as radiation.

(iii) Radiation is the form of light time as the force of light.

(iv) Matter is time.

(v) The magnitude of force is time.

(vi) Matter is the magnitude of force.

Part IV- Matter is Time

(i) Matter is force in time.

(ii) Force is magnitude.

(iii) Light is force without the form of radiation.

(iv) Matter is predicable of form.

(v) Form is not predicable of matter.

(vi) Matter is predicable of radiation.

Diagram

I A ___light___ B
(form of radiation)

II AB (light, force, magnitude)

Appendix

I The representation of space and its objects is an image.

II An abstraction of a proportion of space that posits a consciousness of a conception and its content is a magnitude.

III A system of phenomena that are objects of experience are within a subject of its *Notion*.

Form & Substance—Force & Content:

form is the content of a space

Form is the knowledge of a conditional state of substance in its proximity. Substance in its proximity that is known is conditioned of space where it is of form. Form is infinite of space that a condition of space is infinite of substance. Now substance that has form is infinite of its conditions in space. Conditions in space are infinite of form that they are in infinite representation of form. Then it is that substance is infinite of form where its conditions are in space.

Conditions are formed of space from an infinite substance. Infinity is conditioned of space in its form of substance. Substance is the conditions of space where form is infinitely conditioned. It follows that form is infinite of its conditions of space in infinite motion.

Now matter is the potentiality for the infinite motion of the conditions of space. The conditions of space are in infinite motion where matter has the potentiality for force. It is then that force is a condition of space where matter has form in substance. Form in substance is the force of the matter in space as a condition of motion. It follows that substance is the motion of force in its form as a condition of matter. The conditions of substance are the form of matter where force is a potentiality of the conditions of motion through space. Matter is a condition of space. Matter is a condition of form where space has force. A condition of matter is the form of its content or contents. Space has the condition of matter that concerns the form of force. Form is the content of a space.

Force is the content of a space as a condition of matter. Matter is the force of space in its form of a content. Matter is a content where space has the infinity of form. Space is the necessary condition for the knowledge of form, as it is a content of space. It follows that space is contingent to the content of form. Space is the force of matter contingent to the content of form.(force). Contingent space is the force of matter where form is its content. Form is the content of contingent space. Contingent space is the form of matter in substance. The form of matter in contingent space is in representation of its content. Then it is that force is the representation of matter where space is contingent to the content of form.(contingent representations of force as space—representations of form content from matter in contingent space)

Now a contingent representation is the actuality of a content or contents where force is the form of space. An actual content is actual to the contingency of space where form is the content of a space. It follows that force is the actuality of matter in contingent space in representation of the form of its content. Where space is contingent to the actuality of matter in the form of its content (as force), its actuality has for its content the representation of an actuality of force.(actual motion)—(movables to motion). An actuality of force is in infinite representation of its form in space. As form is infinite of space, form is infinite in its representation of space as the conditions of matter are infinite of form. Now it is that substance is infinite of form in infinite conditional states that are represented in space through these forms.

Magnitudes & Matter-in-itself

Magnitudes in perception as collectives are the object of a Notion, that is the self, though it is in substance collectivity in magnitude, and known as sensation the in-itself of will from otherness; the magnitude of otherness in sensation from will of collectivity. The matter-in-itself is the value of a Notion, in its magnitude of the collective, the totality of the beings-in-themselves in perception of the subject, as magnitude of the will of otherness; that is proportioned commensurable with the conditional value to the collective. This is knowledge as sensation of the collectivity of truth. It is its conclusion in a series of conditions that have been posited into the Object Notion of a subject as a being-in-itself; the repelled in-itself into the Object Notion that is understood within substance at collectivity of value as its circumstance. The value consideration is shuffled in collectivity of substance with the conditions of the subject as Object Notion, and returned in magnitude as conclusion with the content of an action that is in conclusion of the conditions as thought of the subject. This is an a priori conditional truth for the subject that is known *a posteriori* as sensation.

Generality is the conception of an object that is collective in representation of its general Notion, that is the collective of certainty from relations and conception of what is in value consideration the content of an object in proposition to a subject. This holds general value considerations a priori to the object as representative to the collective—in agreement with the value of those general value considerations. It follows that these are held in infinite *regressus* that the being-in-itself is of the generality of the conditions of what are conceptions of an attribute, and never in image-as-representation in an infinite series of representations, that the infinite regressus is of the generality of a set of conditions on properties of beings-in-themselves.[24] It is then recapitulated that images-in-representation are idealist representations, and as phenomena are not known as beings in-themselves contemporaneous with the objects-in-themselves of the same conditions as are presented in the content of the image as representation. However, the image as presented at generality of a particular judgment in a circumstance, and of those conditions, is known as the conception of a subject in the contingency of being; that truth is the general conception at a collective of a proposition in generality—as magnitude is collectively true of the conjoining of forces that are in agreement with a proposition that discloses an event that is then temporalized of the subject; then presented in an image as representation of the contingency of being. Beings-as-collectives are then within the sourcehood of what is contingent of the truth in a magnitude that is of *a priori* conceptions, the knowledge of beings-in-themselves of their identity particulars, and the phenomena of the collective will as the objects as beings-in-themselves are in generality of a contingency of being that is the agreement of a collective truth. This as truth is the generality of the collective will that resolves to the matter-in-itself of a phenomenon that is the collective as objects-in-themselves, in a *regressus* at the conditions of a proposition that is a contingency of being with image representation. That the agreement in the proposition is contingent on the quality of the subject as held within the magnitude of a collective that is both the in-itself of subject and collective as will, in the conditional truth of the image-in-representation that is of a collective will the appropriation of an attribute. For instance, such deception as proliferated through a collective, and realized in the assertion of the

[24] One must of course exercise caution with the casuistry of the concept of matter-in-itself as force, and the properties of beings-in-themselves. As the Self is constituted by an object posited by its own material form, there is no property relation between the image-content and the cogitative material object (substance) constituting subjectivity. For the attribution of the former is attributable to the very act of turning one's self into an object; while the latter is never addressed by the former as a material content to which it stands in property relation addressing the proximate substance of subjectivity—Hegel and Schopenhauer find themselves radically opposed upon this point, respective of the nature of material content in symbolic representations—I would caution that matter be necessarily excluded from form as an ontological condition *a priori* to what appears throughout the latter in order to escape Husserl's ontological "pairing", or worse Hegelian "skull crushing".

totality of being, would have its image-in-representation as the possibility for a subject; and the object-in-itself as it is held in conception of an agreement to the collective that the being-for-itself is contingent to the will. This is also an a priori conception to an analytical judgment of a system of relations that are peripheral to the considerations of a truism in a set of conditions under consideration of the truth, yet the relations as things-in-themselves are of the being-in-itself as situational to an a priori abstraction, that is posited in conception with the image-as-representation rule. It is always that matter-in-itself is in presence as the phenomena of beings-in-themselves, and that the truth is consummated with the will of the collective, at a situation where the truth is relative to a subject-object interplay, that is in the disclosure of an event that is subjectively posited as a spatial abstraction to the positing of magnitude in an abstraction that renders a proposition, and reveals its image-in-representation of an event underway of its posited conditions. This becomes an *infinite regressus* to the will, as it puts truth in agreement with a collective to the being-in-itself, as of the conditioned—which is now the positing of willful objects operating inside the phenomena of a collective in synthetic unity *a priori*. The images-as-representations are causal to the will of the conclusions within *regressus* that are finite to the abstractions that are both ontological properties, and in conception, the image that is an object-in-itself in conception of a spatial abstraction within possibility. Then as truth, the infinity of representations are not of the *Kantian* unconditioned—that an abstraction of a conception through space is of the *Unconditioned*, that the image-as-representation and infinitude in *progressus*, is what is of possibility an abstraction from *the* conditioned. The matter-in-itself in finite and conclusive *regressus* is the appropriation of a quality of being that is causal to the will, and in representation the image of a conception. To further the investigation of this subtle contradiction, it is made in observation that the truth is of the unconditioned that it is not of the will. From causality it is noted, that finite and conclusive *regressus* must also be of the conditioned of its conceptions that are images-in-representation, that the being-in-itself is the finite and conclusive *regressus* of what is necessarily conditional to perception—while the image is of truth as both an abstraction of the horizon of possibility that is of the causality a set of conditioned beings-in-themselves—then it is conceptualized where it is of the unconditioned, an image-in-representation that is the infinity of a *progressus*. This establishes the parallel between image *as* representation, and contemporaneous phenomena that are the wills as beings-in-themselves, that the propositions are in abstraction, properties of matter-in-itself, yet in representation, an image that is perceived of its conditions—though of the unconditioned through an objectification of space. That the temporalization of any given spatial intuition is rendered in a set of conditions that posits an otherness, is that the unconditioned in infinite *regressus* is rendering the spatial qualities of a situation, and that this would be contemporaneous of a certainty that was temporalized of synchronicity, between the matter-in-itself as the collective of wills of phenomena, and the spatial abstraction that gave the image-in-representation its situation in which a contiguous certainty would be discursive with a subject. In this instance the truth would be the absolute of a spatial abstraction, that what was observed were universally true of its image as conditioned, but that the content in observation of the truth as image, would be contingent of the conditions of matter-in-itself. That the image-as-representation is of its spatial abstraction an Absolute Concept, and of the *Unconditioned*, it is of its certainty contemporaneous to the will of matter-in-itself as the phenomena, that is the magnitude of a certainty. That this certainty is within an Absolute of Truth that is its spatial temporalization, it is a condition to the will that is its point of sufficient reason; where the magnitude of a condition is realized in a phenomenal will and in image *representation*. That this as certainty is conditional of truth, it is yet of the Absolute of Truth in its unconditioned of space as a temporalization—where the judgment from an observation based on analytical judgments has made the image-as-representation of a judgment absolute in reality, as it is contiguous with the phenomenal will as matter-in-itself. Though for this, it is still that causality of the conditioned, is its own existent of matter-in-itself as the possibility of unconditional truth; where an unconditioned that is the spatial abstraction that is known from a *progressus* from existing conditions, would only be known of unconditioned space, that the conditions would be of truth. However, these conditions are as effects the *regressus* from the point in space where the unconditioned is the causality of what is in its effects a temporalization articulated in the conditions as effects. This suggests yet again that the images are of truth in the unconditioned as possibility, though are subject to the conditions of the will in judgments and certainties within phenomena. Again, what is contemporaneous to the will as phenomena in magnitudes of contingencies of being as collectives, are the contiguous posits as conceptions of a circumstance, but that the content of a phenomenon with its image-in-representation, must be contemporaneous with the matter-in-itself to be known as reality; other than its possibility in a situation where its content were from conditions to the will. That the image is of possibility from the unconditioned, and of the conditions of the will apprehended, it is of these conditions that the matter-in-itself may be known. That the phenomenon is of third party otherness in the conditions to the will it is not yet of truth, and the contemporaneous knowledge of the subject as being-in-itself is yet of the will in pursuit of truth; though of *a priori* judgments truth is unconditioned, and absolute in the knowledge of the being-in-itself. The unconditioned that is in *progressus* of human judgments, that are conditions in a given situation for the pursuit of truth, is the contingency of truth in an unconditioned Absolute that is the potentiality of the conditioned Absolute of a being-in-itself.[25] The Absolute of Truth is never contingent on the truth of its conditions at the in-itself, and therefore Will in its Absolute of Truth knows the in-itself of its conditional Absolute, that is the unconditioned of an infinite series, that penetrates beings-in-themselves of an unconditioned Absolute; through the proximity as established of a set of "conditions as judgments" which disclose attributes from actuality and from conditions to the will. These proximities are from possibilities as conditioned, finitely available in representations, as they are infinite of their conditions as possibilities toward the unconditioned; that space is infinite in *progressus,* unless it is of the necessary conditions to the will—a being-for-itself. That beings-in-themselves might become matter-in-itself—yet known in representation from the conditioned an infinite series to the unconditioned, the *regressus* is a condition or set of conditions to a certain point in space as *Being*—this is the conditional truth that is true of its conditions to the knowledge of a being-in-itself; from a proximity that is conclusive of that set of conditions as a confirmation of the truth in a possibility. Where horizons of possibility are transcendences of the spatial context from where content had emerged—posited through the conditions of an objectification of images, as propelled from their positions in abstract possibility (infinite *regressus*)—there may be nothing of material content within the images as ontological forms. For those that are posited within the space of representation as abstractions to the being-in-itself, that Schopenhauer

[25] Note the unconditioned of Kant in Schopenhauer's dialectical will to sustain a Hegelian being-in-itself possessing absolute knowledge.

posits in essence as matter-in-itself, and Hegel *force*; material content that had been ontologized into conceptual forms that could be abstracted from their horizontal positionality, must continue to remain independent from the representational forms as objects, images, and noumenal presentations of a will. While the subjective will benefits from contingent articulations of self-identity, the reflexive modality of material form would otherwise become radically jeopardized.

Chapter 2 Mind and Machine, Nature and Technology

That pressure systems are relative of the elements within a given space, these systems are known from intuition in their proportion of space in the force of pressure that is present within another space, relative to the proportion of space from where the initial element of space exists. This is a cognitive ability that derives the mechanical force of a pressure system and converts it into a relative mathematical figure that identifies its relative pressure, in relation to the surrounding proportions. The instruments for measuring these relative proportions of space are human-made, and are utilized to change the quality of an element in space, with the employment of another element. Such as is the correlation between fire, or heat, air (with all its considerable properties contingent of geologically present gaseous chemicals), water, and earth (that its continents contain chemicals that are heated and evaporate into the air (petroleum, fossil fuels)). These instruments, such as are everything in consideration of thermodynamics, from household furnaces and ventilation ducts to jet engines, are all to be classified within what will be called a *thermological* system. [26]

When we consider the presence of a hydrocarbon in the atmosphere, seldom do we grow suddenly frightened, or begin to derive suspicions that something may be wrong with this presence, as it is something we know and use to our domestic advantage and know as natural gas. We cook with it, heat our homes with it, and expect that it performs at all times safely, and poses no threat to human safety at any time. That this is a naturally produced product of fossil fuels, we can also expect that it is able to do much more than simply provide us with household convenience, as in its

---

[26] A proprietary term making reference to the conditions causal to an interaction between human substances of being, and substances such as fossil fuels—and the mind's reflexive responses to both where conditional of *being*.

immediate association to petroleum, the universality of the motor vehicle's presence is brought to mind—as in consideration of what might also be the most important thermological machine under consideration. The important thought here is the knowledge of the existence of a by-product, and its pollutant waste, resultant of the use of petroleum, and how it interacts with the presence of other fossil fuels. The instant association to make is that we most definitively have motion, where considers this highly available and utilized substance. To begin with this in consideration of substance, will be the goal of the following investigation into the associative possibilities of what the exterior presence of various fossil fuels in the atmosphere and within machines as thermological systems can do for the movability of properties within substance.

Firstly, since all that is matter is of carbon at its base, and this is the base element of all matter, it follows that anything compound that was also of carbon—bonded in a molecule with another agent—would possess the essential qualities to bond with another molecule of its base, that the second agent was also in a universal state. It is observed here that the presence of hydrogen in the air, is of necessary universality, such as would make its carbon companion equally mobile. We might consider identifying this combination as the fuel of substance, rather than substance itself.

Theoretically, we may posit a topological filiation between motor vehicles and consciousness, and will here find that the manifold of relations, is very much within the *machinery* of consciousness, such as is the manifold in an automobile; and that the systems that apply to both of these in comparison, are not too dissimilar that the humor likening physicians to glorified mechanics is merely a opportunity to insure silence—in consideration of adequate and appropriate emergency health care. The principle at work in this instance, will be called the principle of contemporaneous motion. This stipulates that objects in motion of their elemental trajectory, are relative to rectilinear motion in trajectory of a subject-object property of substance; that it is perceived in relative motion, that the quality of motion of an object from force, is superior to the force of motion of a object of its quality; that it is held in connection with force as an object through space in possession of an attribute that is held as a movable (object Notion). In perceived space, the object stands in relation to the subject, that the object is both machine and subject in relation to another subject of its Object Notion; and the perceived motion in relation as a set of conditions in the proportion of space as substance, represents the relative movability of an Object Notion—that is a property of substance. The subject-within-machine object that is in relative motion to another subject, is in relation to the thermological component of substance that is of its base-as-compound the particularity of substance, that the conception of a motion through space relative to a subject, has this subject in relative conception of its motion, and that the base-as-compound is within this being as relative of its motion to a universality of substance from a thermological system—the necessary proportion of a particular quality or a set of qualities. In this relation, it is that we might also identify the human artifice as another thermological system, such as would be relevant to the stoics or Tinman.

A contemporary example of this principle is the Hell's Angels. The mobility of substance is only chased sufficiently by a perpetually travelling motorcycle; lest the discomfort of unrelenting appropriation begins to settle in.

Force and Nature

The force of nature can be a vicious and uncompromising "act of God" that destroys much of the beauty that is created through its essence. These events seem to be precipitous of the unknown, yet phenomenal magnitudes of Nature that compel us to wonder at the origins of cause, as they act within us to search deeper into the meaning to the order of nature. Precisely what does generate these necessary chemical equations in the formation of Nature, and the manner by which things interact naturally fascinates us to every extreme. We have always concluded that occurrences that are as interminable mysteries to us, have always been random occasions, when the variables of this system collide in a force that is as tragic as it is beautiful.

Our world is separated from the essence of a natural causal order, while contained within each occurrence of Nature that continues to supply us with a new sense of amazement. We allow the occasions of Nature to define the way we think and the way we feel. What we often fail to conclude, is how we think is to a large degree with what is in its effects—the order of Nature; that our civilization can interact with an ecosystem outside of the direct impact our culture has on its ordinance of an ecological well-being. The immediacy of our culture in its interconnectedness is subject to a natural law, and within this its Causality defines the inter-dynamical system that organizes these societal infrastructures; while attempting to modify the course of immutability in the order of these events, through the sophistications of media and cultural industry. That the by-products of these systems of organization produce waste that interacts with ecosystems, has always been an identifiable problem, one that has been issued at the forefront of most ecological concerns, along with the jeopardization of the natural habitats of endangered species; yet our natural practices in relation to these systems has never been clearly revealed to the population as what is most paramount in this sense of alarm. We protect our freedoms and manage our actions with an acuity that supplies an ever-evolving culture, with as securely convenient a standard of living as can be found anywhere else on the planet. What we are facing is the reason that affects this security within our natural habitat, as it does the order of Nature in the endangerment of other species, working through the midpoint of cultures that reveal those that are more directly intertwined with Nature; as Nature is in consideration of a higher power in the order of the world of Nature as is God. When we consider a Genus—a superior force that orders the genera of a species and articulates the essential qualities of organisms—species and plant life—we consider what is within the nucleus of the life-force generated in the continuation of these life forms, and how its ability to adapt to the environment is conditional with how it interacts with other species or life forms. This consideration marks the fundamental human apprehension toward what is causal of things within the totality of Nature and our world, as we move toward a greater understanding of the significance of our being within them; and our ability to protect other life forms around us as we would our own. When we look after ourselves, it is essential that we observe what waste we put into nature, not only of our culture industry, but what we allow to affect the sources of existence; what generates life forms and continues throughout history. We have already been supplied with the knowledge that our actions are not directly generative of a force capable of interfering with this Genus, but that as a foregone conclusion of the first beginning of evolutionary life, humanity's resource was tooled after what would improve the conditions of this existence, and that the essential quality of life would follow—given that humans evolved contingent to these developmental sophistications. Yet it would seem that human technologies have outlasted the mysteries in the generation of new life forms, and that our abilities to synthesize the human artifice, commiserate with our abilities to action against the better health of these origins, were generated from Causality of our existence as essences. What is actioned in our relation to Nature, is directly proportional to what is relational of our action toward the generation of our own species within Genus; what would first be identified as the hidden source of a disease, then articulated within the body as a full blown ailment of varying degrees. How we wrong each other, is how we act on what is pro-generative of the species as a whole, yet manufactures a particular benefit to those able to transcend the short pitfalls of disease with the prompt attention of a physician—though we would claim that ultimately this is solvent to the necessities of what is denominational within disease; in that its odds are precipitant of both what is generated of substance, and of what is interpreted by the genetic chronology of the human artifice, in relation to the proportions of health available to others. What does occur within human action, that is represented in consciousness of a genera that it is not a first principle of genera—yet a relational configuration of the relative health of objects in a system of our manifold—is directly proportioned with the potentiality of a being toward health or a being toward disease; based both on the ability to interpret being as such, and on the congenital predispositions that predicate of those ontological conditions as present within these genera, as a tertiary principle of being of genera within consciousness. A great source of concern, is how our actions may influence the relational properties of a genera, that in a totality of being as a species, we have been maximized of what is available within Genus of a species; that human attributes are now defined only by our action, and never by their congenital proximities. Where we make this a manufacture of equanimity that is synonymous with freedom in a culture, we risk the influence of other cultures responsive to what is pro-generative of a species, and find ourselves looking toward these cultures under the wrong circumstances, those that reveal the terminal ends of our actions as a species, and those that displace our sense of knowledge. We find ourselves bearing witness to suicide and ritual sacrifice each day, without the realization that this sacrifice is articulating the removal of a freedom that is within these as finitude in-itself, a freedom to enter the land of God where Genus is not being tampered with by any human technology that is destructive to the greater well-being of a global species. It is that we consistently address the danger that this poses to us, in that it reveals a stark and pronounced disregard for human life, from the standpoint of those destroyed in innocence; and without justifiable reason an act that has no pronounced impetus, other than to destroy what is within the path of this as a force of nature; a magnitude of explosive intention than wishes to articulate the violence of privation with a mechanical human machinery—a system of technology representative of one of the many interferences that plague a consciousness in its freedom, without the cultural responsibility that identifies these cultural end points—the spiritual societies that are assembled in direct fellowship with a consciousness that is predicable of this Genus. It is this as a human freedom—in all of its power—that humanity's conduct is put before the contents of what is known as causal within Nature.

That our humanity is imparted to us of a nature, that our relation to objects we encounter and perceive is realized in this humanity—the point of reference to which everything is received within us in its vitality or in its serenity—is the emotionality of our being. The innate ability to consciously reflect on our relational being, or to encounter the dynamics of nature as within any systematic configuration of life with any sense that is of the quality of the experience, is the potentiality to react to the inherent beauty of all things within Nature; and to have a sense of disgust at the ferocity and ruthlessness of events that sometimes take place. It is that we are more commonly taken with this radiance, than we are within its potential power of destruction. We continue to pursue the quietude of the natural environment that allows us to escape the pressures of the industry culture; the compulsory mandate of each citizen to fulfill obligations as part of the social order. This is so much the case that society itself begins to possess its own natural order—an order of Nature. With all this, daily interactions and encounters, that would invariably total up to a cacophony of chaotic incoherence, in all the traffic—it seems that there is this order. A combination of forces that combine to form the patterns of existence within causation—a technological assembly of mechanized reality that becomes of the collectivity of action—a natural authority in the course of events that organizes each moment as it relates to the next. That we have already identified the presence of technology and its controls, it is also necessary to observe the inherent significance of what is causal from

Nature, in the pursuit of a greater understanding of the proportions of our psyches, that may order Nature to interact with any human made device. The technological machinery of the mind has developed its imagination, it has evolved and fabricated these devices that are able to perform tasks once only performed by humans. It has projected itself into those machines with the idea of what it does, a furtherance in the imagination that displays how machines articulate our human wills. We design our realities to suit our needs, and as these are realized we *will* to effectuate changes around us that would enable our existence further. Each piece of the puzzle in the design of our own species, is already known to us—that it can repair itself and heal—and this same knowledge is available to us within the designs of what we make. What disassembles our cognition of these abilities, is what empowers the greater strength of a corporate industry, to maintain these technologies separate of our existence; but what exists for us within these is how we are involved with them in our daily lives, and how our mere perception of these as objects other than human beings, have been built into our existence—replacing some of the direct considerations we once had with a convenience that is its own set of new considerations. Where we facilitate daily life to this extreme, we take all of facility within existence and deliver it the singular problem, of a non-facilitated essence within existence. We incapacitate the urgings of a life driven by unpredictability and spontaneity, to perfect life's process from a technological point of view. We are possessed with the knowledge of a facility and its perfection; that is causal of behavioral effects in an imposition upon us, the efficiency that is correlative of this technological facility. Just as problems within equipment impose upon us this threat toward a perfect efficiency, our humanity is troubled with the imperfection of the facility of process, to discover that no longer is our human functionality optimal. In essence, we have evolved psychically within an industry culture, to manage the convenience of facility within our souls.

A material object is both in representation its idea, as it is in its actuality the thing itself. Its representation presents to us color and form, and its relational qualities: the aspects of the existing qualities as they interact with other properties of matter. That this representation presents to us the thing as an idea, our sense of space and distance dictates how these qualities are perceived both in relation to other objects, but also to the idea itself or form, which is to be apprehended as the temporality of an object in representation.

The force and functionality of a thing or object brings to us in actuality, an object as existent through the empirical laws of Nature. The qualities of an object—other than the ones that are perceived—are apparent to us only in consideration of how we may relate to it, and how we may utilize its functionality for our own purposes. These are functional conditions of a thing—that is, they are the conditionality, where they refer to us in our state and alter it, of its inherent conditionality through what is effectual of our action causal of this dynamic. This suggests that we are approaching the idea of a thing, and acting on it, that our relation to it is one that is causal. The manner in which these objects present themselves to us as ideas, is also causal of our perception of these things as ideas—in that we do not have knowledge of them *a priori*, yet that they are still in existence of their idea or form. It follows that as ideas in thought, these things already in existence, are now thought as ideas in their effects, put in touch with our a priori sense of knowledge before existence. That with our intuitions of space, we can know these objects as the content of a space, as the a priori ideas that are the contents of a space or spaces; where a thing not yet in existence is formed of an existing space, that its contents are not yet known. Now the representations of these ideas may be other ideas than the ones that are perceived, where form is the content of its ideas. Those things that simply are, the matter of which is found in all considerations of what is Nature herself, of all its botanical life, yet without species and the elements themselves that are also in representation of the idea, before the actuality that is Nature itself. Where this is so represented of its actuality, is through the phenomena that Nature offers, announcing its presence to us sometimes without warning, yet always with an antecedent to the cause. These are *synthetic* occurrences, unities of various overlapping elements that combine in what is considered a natural system, [27] and represents another synthesis of unities that are correlates of relational properties of matter; that are its modality. A cloudy day is a mode of Nature, where the unities of clouds have combined to form a grey sky rather than a blue sky on a sunny day. The combination of natural modes, element unity and non-coalescence that exist within nature, storms for instance, and the

[27] Natural in the sense that it is largely based upon energies supplying the general existence of organisms that are subject to the environment in which they exist—as either sustainable or unsustainable essences.

functionality of these relative to the greater ecosystem, constitute the truth of Nature; that is the Absolute of the totality of events that are ordered in its relational qualities, constitutive of the potentiality of an occurrence from its effects of a causality.

The matter within the actuality of Nature is what is known of its representation from sense, yet the phenomena of Nature is known in-itself of the force of Nature as its content matter-in-itself. The water within clouds during a rainstorm, is perceived in the form of a phenomena that is a rain shower; yet we are identifying another state of the matter which is the clouds as things in-themselves. That these phenomena also present to us an idea, and a set of circumstances that are conditions of aspects of a functionality within Nature, identifies its determinateness[28] in modality. That this is in its effect a change in determinateness, resultant of a unity or movement within its previous state, identifies the conditionality of motion in a determinateness to the elements of Nature. In consideration of form as the temporality of an idea in Nature, with one element of Nature in motion of its idea that is the change in determinateness, it is that one determinateness of its change in determinateness in relation to another determinateness, are both in motion of their idea; as is form the temporality of a thing within Nature. Where two ideas in a multiplicity of Nature are within a determinateness what is relational—with the change in determinateness of a motion of one element of Nature—is the motion of a determinateness in another element of Nature, that its idea as a determinateness is of matter more than it is of form. These may be considered the representations that are contemporaneous of the dynamical conditions of other exterior representations that are their determinateness.

Representations and Notionality

A representation that is the idea of a thing, object, being, or quality in its determinateness, also has for it a content in a judgment or proposition. Its form is temporality that is a change in determinateness that signifies a

[28] The concept defines what is characteristic of the metaphysics of Aristotle, while in contemplation of a Spinoza's monism—bound into the modal consequentialism of Kant. Since, this duality presupposes an objective relation, it is modal to the conditions of something that commands a necessary unified ontological field.

movement that is of a contrary property or relational in differentia—the object in a representation of a certainty. The conditional representation of contingent beings, is an a priori awareness of an object of relational beings—dynamically contemporaneous with other exterior representations. That content is form—it is phenomena of a magnitude when in the relative temporality of its relational differentia. The phenomenal magnitude of a collectivity in representation, is the relative temporality of all associated contingents as things-in-themselves; of their temporal mass in distance with force as a constant.

It is within observance that for its causality, emotionality has what reveals in its effects an act of privation what may evoke the tears of an enduringly helpless woman. That nature can be cruel without appearance of reason—that it may violate the soul—it is issued of what forces collide in an occurrence conclusive of a unity that has shed its contrariness in an irrevocably stark moment of determinateness, that is fueled of what appears an individual certainty; though precisely what descends into the action of an individual that pursues the conditions of a particular cause from its effects—that are the basis of an outcome that is an immutability of Nature—the contingent relational being. This is contemporaneous with the conditions of a phenomena in its content, that is the *truth* of the relational being. The contingency of being as phenomena has for its content of cultural beings, a contemporaneous relational truth in the contingency of being.

This is paradigmatic of objective relational beings, and it is contemporaneous with noumenal subjects. This promulgates a necessity of truth that is the coalescence in a circumvention of relational contexts contemporaneous with cultural being, as it does correlate relational beings to paradigms. Cogitatively, this presumes that things themselves are in an inherence of relation, where concerns the immediacy of what is structured of a priori relations; that beings appear in their form and content with both representations and contingencies, that are in a contiguous dynamical interplay that designates the temporality of phenomena. From the standpoint that the necessary dynamical conditions of inter-related contingencies make this designation, it is causal of the magnitude of this dynamical content that it is in circumvention—with both the a priori representations and their cultural contingencies, of which are actualities in exterior representations, then responsive to the circumventive process—while at hand in an a priori representation that is conditional. This conditional representation is entirely contiguous with a thing-in-itself, that is available to a privation with a cultural sufficiency in reason. The Notionality is conditionally associated with what is etymologically presented, as it is with what is virtual in the certainty of things that are its influence.

What is spatial of these influences is dynamic of its spatiality. Of its inherence it is exteriority itself, in that its representation of space in presence is supervenient to the direct representation of space, contingent to the influence of a content—this the technological representation. That this content is also as phenomena beings-in-themselves, these beings are both contingencies as they are actualities—then identifiably the particular beings in representation; that they are also conditional with the dynamics in presentation of their relevance of content. That a contingency of being is now in exteriority, the actuality of beings-in-themselves is antecedent to the causation of an actuality of phenomena, that has for its content the dynamical conditions of this as an actuality in its proximity. This actuality is of its proximity, the logical circumvention of a conditional being, that its contingency is now in actuality. Of its conditions that are determinateness, it reflects the a priori existence of what are essences in their fabrication, conditional of an actuality that is differential to the reified presence, which is a contingent actuality to an actuality, now in contrariness to the differentia of the contingent actuality; with the actuality in a differential determinateness to its own contingency. Further to this, it is that with this as contingency in its actuality, that its representation is actual of a contingent actuality—the subject to the contingency of actuality must also have its contingency to its own actuality. This is a dynamical unity of contingencies for beings-in-themselves, that is relational to the phenomena of a things-in-representation, depicted in a medium that is a technology of its media. That these contingencies are also certain of their conditions in relation—where the relational dynamic is fused with a virtual dynamic of the conditionality of things as beings that posit substance—there is a dynamical inter-relation between actualities and contingent necessities that are both actual and virtual.

Actualities and Virtualities

Where we act on contingencies, we act as virtualities. [29] That everything essential is an actuality—yet without the knowledge of its contingency—it is that its virtual presence is known as an actuality in its *Being*. This is of its certainty the presence that is known of its conditions that are representationally signified, more than it is known in the context of its signification. The being itself is known as contingency, where it is represented in the content that is framed within the circumstance of a relation, where it is the source of influence of a contingently actual being, then also a conditional entity in enterprise with an actual contingency; also it is the representation of being which is fictitious in its nature, and is now represented in a certainty that is actual of its conditions where concerns the virtual being—now represented in the Being of actuality. There is a relation that has been encumbered with the relationality of a contingency that is technologically biased, as superseded by the incurrence of wisdom that was made in the deliverance of a currency—that is upon its circumvention—the value of a virtual being in the actuality of a conditional certainty, upon which the inter-connectedness of a collateralized entity is juxtaposed in an a priori expectancy to the conditionality of the unconditioned subject. This is the infinity of technological expectancy, in consequence to the actual technology that is multifarious in representation.

That I might reproduce an eternity for one moment, I reproduce one moment for an eternity.

Everything that has form, is Other to content that its space represents. Everything that is space without content is of form, that it has been represented through space. Things that are infinite of form are infinite of space.

---

[29] The context into which this is posited or expressed, is one that is more concerned with the consciousness of ontological explorations—rather than becoming virtual in the sense of a commodification of Self in the neural network of a bio-technological transformation.

Images of objects that are finite of form in representation, are infinite of space in a content. Each movement that is represented in form, is form in the representation of a movement.

Reciprocity within Nature from Contingencies

& The Technological Contingent Being

Relational beings that have contingencies are within dynamics whereby the contingency of one being, becomes of the determinateness of another being; that is the reciprocal force of a nature between two contingencies. When in a subject, the property that is contained of its contingency in representation of an object that is its image, it is of reciprocity that the object itself is the possibility to a subject. This possibility is of its certainty in a contingency—the awareness of the object in the possibility of a subject, that it has been represented to the object in an image. As a reciprocity in determinateness, it is that properties are within the representation of a contingency of its content, that the determinateness of the subject is now placed in representational proximity to the object, where it is now a possibility of the subject, rather than an actuality of its own determinateness. Here the form in representation to the subject is the actual movement of the object, such as its movement a change of state in relation to its situational space. This identifies what is of motion, such as an individual that walks through a room, or an idiosyncrasy: that is a sudden affectation or tic that is peculiar to the awareness—as constitutes the necessary conditional change that is a movement in a state of being. For these, there is a content of a representation that is conditional to particularity; where the contingency of a being is contained within an instrument that expresses its proximal conditions in relation to another being, as unconditioned of this being, yet in motion of a determinateness that is a priori now in proximity of the object rather than of the subject. The conditionality of a subject is relational to a force of nature that is pure consciousness of a collectivity, in an infinity of a particular conditional collective that is for the object its influence.

That determinateness in representation to the subject of its object is the possibility of motion—in that it has been placed in a natural relation to what is relative of motion, and that this dynamical relation is infinite to what is possible of a subject, toward an object already in motion. That this relation is observed of the subject, and that the determinateness of the subject is in motion of the object, that the subject has an awareness of the object in perception, it is never synthetic to the determinateness of the subject. This is not a control of influence, yet it is a control that is of the observation that there has been a relocation of purposiveness of the sheer observance of motion, thereby consecrating the relation of subject-object, as though in an assignment of capabilities *a priori*; that is not dissimilar to the designation that is made of humans and technology as a observational mechanism. Of this claim it is that the immediacy of the presence of an instrumentation in thought, that is infinite to the conditions of an individual as a representation of a contingency of being, is simply of this as though algorithmic in its instrumentation; as it as resolves to a technological contingency in an finitude that is expressed in a medial form, rather than a representation that is an aural conveyance. Within the advancement of thought, it may be considered that this is to be classified as a certainty, and each other instrumentation of objective thought is to be known as a contingency, relative to the organically dynamical and technologically limited forms of knowledge, that are represented to the abstract mind.

When we consider the Newtonian law of motion that is inertia, it is noted that we must now introduce the consideration of what is contingency of being, as it *is* within a medium of thought. This is not as yet, a mode of consciousness, but presents within the notion of movement, the notion of reciprocal movement from contingent forms of media, that are as newly presented modes of consciousness. What this suggests is that the motion of a content through a medium, is within a relational inertia with a content in its form. It also posits that a content in its form is within a medium. Now that a medium can be thought, or within forms of knowledge, it is that its phenomena is represented in the medium itself. That this media knows no movement—other that its actual circulation—it is that it is in collective representation in a contingency of motion from circulation. Its logical circumvention is that from its own collectivization, its motion is inherent of the representation; though it is based within the referent that is its collective proximity. This is now what will be considered a technological ecosystem, that it has bound from one source of its media; the origins of a collectivization that is in contingent movement with its circulation. This acts in accordance with the laws of nature that necessitate equal reciprocal movement—these may circumvent its force, firstly within the spheres encompassing its generality of movement; and secondly whereby the properties are in contingencies that are facilitated of the collectivization of an inertial media distribution—further engaged by the dynamical synthesis of properties, available through the media possibilities. These are only in a general circumvention of their collectivization from facticity, though these are empowered within a general reciprocal movement of equal and opposite force—in relation to the very conception of those; yet that they are now incidental to the conditional magnitudes. These magnitudes are now in stasis of the circumvention that is the relational movement of a content in its form. It is now the connectivity of motion is necessitated of its *Unconditioned*;[30] that is the state of a body at rest before it has become of its motion. This is the first principle of the technological contingent being.

This is a human technology that is its nature, it designs the soul in its likeness that is reproductive of humanity that is infinite in its conception. The species resolves to the most contemporary notion of reproduction, where it considers its motional ability to design and manufacture what it already knows to exist. The obscure sense of what is its existence from what is a general state of being, is the absence of a direct and all-encompassing knowledge of the interconnectedness of things. This is *prima facie* to the recognition of one such interconnectedness as is our technological understanding. The sense in which our collective knowledge is presented to us. That we are now also in another natural relation, is what considers further the forms in our faculties of knowledge; and how they may intermingle with other elements of Nature.

When we think of information in its Universality, we first think of light. This is the source of all our circumspections, the connecting element in the universe that reveals to us that which we might know.

---

[30] Here posited in contrast to Kant's unconditioned. Ibid., p 20. The concept that the essential content of horizons of consciousness, are realized as objects of thought—delivering the notion of a reality bound to a dialectic centered within the dynamics of the Hegelian possibility/impossibility philosophic aporia.

When we consider for a moment that information is entirely given of light, and that we are creatures that are primarily motivated by knowledge—in all of its forms of intuition and discovery—then we may instantly think of the process that is photo synthesis: the process whereby plants convert light into compound sugars as a source of nutrition. This demonstrates that plants are performing a bio-chemical activity that is dealing with what is to us, also a source of information in another state; and that this process has been so entitled. It suggests that the nutritive process of the vegetation—and with its life force that is in dealing with this process—is also capable of a contingency that is within another state of light. That it *is* light, an information carrier, it follows that contingencies as images are possibilities of vegetation, and they are life forms that are connected to other like life-forms that utilized the same process in their process of survival. Where we consider that the plant is absorbing its light, and as nutrition that the light itself is informed of the form of a plant that it has illuminated—that the plant is visible to us by this very illumination—it is that the light it has reproduced of the plant itself is in presence to us and is so visible to us, in the possibility of a reproduction in thought; considered an object of the imagination, yet contingent to its actuality—that only those things that are actual to the conception that is blended with the organicness of the plant, are contemporaneous with its light possibility, or will be visible. It appears that the forms of the imagination are immediate of a pure synthesis of the imagination, that is reproduced organically.

The form that is organic, that has reproduced an object in its content in that it is in form, is the natural contingent of a relational object. This is that an object may be known of another life form in proximal representation through the understanding. Unlike teleology however, this is in consideration of botanical life forms that are the information carriers of objects of the pure understanding. This proportions the human in connection with the ecosystem of a similar teleology, as other species within Nature, that are driven instinctually by the order of Nature, defining their survival patterns within the elements. In relations of the hunter and the hunted, it is that the hunter is more prone to its endangerment than the hunted, as its survival depends on the prey:—the predator of species is in jeopardy and never hunts merely for sport, and the hunted species escapes the predator—for it has strengthened its nature and moved to a renewed state of its evolutional resource. The species that do not develop this resource invariably become of extinction, as the predatorial nature of a survival-obsessed species, is in reduction of those very resources that reproduce the ecological inter-dynamics; such as were the case with dinosaurs:—though it is this grand extinction that has donated our current supply of natural energy that are fossil fuels; — the very resource of our struggle based within a survival quest that recaptures these historical dynamics, civilized by the sciences that practiced resource control as a function of responsible commerce within the greater economical system.

When we find ourselves connected to the apparatus—rather than to our souls—it is that we reconstitute our selves through perceptual abilities—signified as glimpses into a wandering soul, more through a bio-ecological organic means; of an existence that is Universal of its essence, as is within Nature the reciprocity in force that expresses its determinateness in other aspects of the same system. The state in which we consistently assigned portions of the self to its technological ends, as significations of societal existence: we are locked in to an essence that is within the governance of their systems—yet powered of the will to transcend their boundaries at an increasingly provisional rate, positing the substance of a secured performance as individuated cultural factions. Herein contains a certain natural indebtedness, that reflects the commerce of a political social system—opposing the reconstituted Self of Nature. Of this as an indebtedness, is that all transactions in pursuit of the amends that may be irreconcilable within pure reason, are a privation that is licensed of an immaterial valuation—never supervenient to substance in its value, that is legalized and collectively adhered to. What this posits in principle, is the dynamical collectivity of a currency that is realized from ontological relations—a sense of value that is commensurable with transactions that are present in the daily economy of its actual operations. Subsequently, all movement of currency that is taking place within the economy, is also taking place in substance—that it is maintained within reason in its indebtedness or particularity that is weighted with the dynamical distribution of a currency that is of some edification, such as within a corporate body. The vagueness in a mandate that is the norm with any such corporate entity—as is in interest of currency that is investment currency or an alike sum that is derived of a projected actuality—is in consideration here for not in its policy; but in its pragmatism that is the conduct of the individuals and groups instrumental in application of a dynamical currency. Eventually the issue here becomes one of the relative health of an economy, versus the relative health of a species. Where movement is considerably defined by groups in concern with the maintenance of a material currency within reason—then continually based on its designs in the abundance of proximity to a substance in an essentiality of its value—there is a dogmatic contradiction within the practice of reason, that endangers the greater health of a reason based culture; whereby movables are being set within substance that is pro-generative of the species of its health, and clustered into what eventually becomes an essentiality of disease. From where we concern ourselves with a modern utility, it suggests that the eventuality of disease is that it is contiguous with the movement of a currency, that is relative of substance to the economy in its daily practices accrued over a period of time.

Now if a culture considers each of its subjects, both with the equal potentiality for long lasting health as for the eventuality of disease, that it has made all properties contingent on the dynamics of a commerce-driven cultural engine, then it has suggested that the quality of existence is to be governed of material currency practices that are ethical. That is, all those that pay are never to be forgiven their practices beyond reason, as these are clearly defined by those that are within the very practices of commerce. What is given of this is the convenience of a Genus-principled bank account, that consistently ensures the permanence of substance—as it is that the exchange-value has been of notice secured within the naturally perpetuated record of what allows for selective survival within a system; that has been technologized along with the stratifications within the economy. The action that is a mounting of properties significant of material wealth—yet indifferent of proximity, is a practice that robs the wealthy of spirit of their natural inheritance of substance—and not positing enjoyment of Universality within consciousness.

Media currency and the responsible being of ownership

What presents me my currency is my objects. Though that these are a determinateness that is mine—as it is in representation to me—it is also that in its basis is found the movement of a currency that is material, and never what is imagined from conceptions. What is also in representation here are references to actualities, that are not of substance or of any currency whatsoever. These are mere perversions that remove from essence, for an existence deprived of its instruments and ontological possibilities. However, these are dynamical of any source of representation that is in relation to a subject of its conditions; and consecrates the discontinuation of any magnitude of thought, within the contemporaneous relevance that makes this its cultural end—rather than the collectivization of perceptions found in the represented magnitude of thought. This acts from what is causal of truth, toward what are the ends in their effects that further circumvent the currency equation through a commonality of informational referents.

The being-for-itself that makes a claim on the entirety of a totality of being—which is ever-present in perception in a temporality that relates a property and properties to a thing—then becomes of functionality what is a public utility. The paradox of thought that contemplates an ordinance, or an existence before essence that is the soul of consciousness, with its facticity supervenient to nothingness *in lieu* of a transcendent apprehension of universals and absolutes, then are as existents found within the same claim that is administrable within a facticity. [31] It is here that we discover a municipal directive that is implemented of the requirements of the greater population, as conditioned with the necessities of the citizens. This is inclusive to what propels an economy of its cultural requirements, toward what is acceptable to a public that has been contained within those requirements. If the basis of a culture is trade, or it is freedom, what is compromised in facticity as an existence is the universality of value. The currency is kept standard in its material form, yet it is trading in other proportions that are contemporary with the acceptable practices that are considered freedoms. Our intentionality in the legalization of a set of proprieties, is nothing dissimilar with what would be more ethical within our practices of reason; for the benefit of what are within cultural practices, that are causal in the development of media technologies—will eventually influence minds toward their own personal evolutions. The process incurrent of a reflective cultural influence is a degradation and devolution of thought itself; that it is no longer antecedent to the experience of a culture, but a mere reproduction

[31] The concept of universals or absolutes to the facticity of *Sartre*, exudes a considerable sense of what must be posited subjectively through an existential transcendence of human becoming.

of the conflicts and resolutions that are found within these forms of communications. A logical circumvention is not a choice that is a freedom to the individual, yet it is the freedom to choose. The desire to be free is a liberty to perform without administrable restrictions—as that which is already made of consumptive fabrication, is represented to populations of its symbolic messaging. What a cultural work represents, is less intentional than a solution to the problem—rather than the problem itself within its fabrication. Yet that we are dynamically associated in conjunction with its media, it is that the solutions must be known in their actualities to subjects; not in mere representations of what are solutions to an unknown problem that is never dealt with. This presupposes the magnitude of media influence—in that it is dealing with a problem that is in turn mounting a new set of conditions within consciousness. These problems are the actualities of beings-for-themselves; that are not understood as contingent beings to the subjects for whom these problems that have been installed, of a cultural circumvention that has now become the content of pure fabrications,—that are in turn presented once again with the judgments that are found the content of a subject once again. As we are suppressing the exterior behavior of the population, we are mounting the necessary components within consciousness that reflect those ideas, as demonstrable within their cultural reifications.

That objects are media is being. The essential quality of a being, is that the individual within this which is being, is both object and entity, that is the totality of the historicity of what is this which is being. When we know an entity, it is both the representation of this which is expected of knowledge, as this which is concurrent of being to an entity. The entity that is within being is known of what is contemporary of knowledge—where concerns the being that is cognizant of an existence that apprehends the being that is specifically in apprehension of an essence—within an accordance of the very existence that is being; of the apprehends that are within being, contemporaneous with the representations that are *Being*. The system requires this being for its apprehension that *gives* its being, such that its presence is submitted to the apprehends of being—as this which is to be known as suchness,—for the purposes of what is to be construed as this which is desired. It would be so revealed that this suchness is to be interpreted as is—such that it would be designated within the apprehends of being; the pursued *thisness*—which is the sameness of the others in contemporaneity: which is as though the subjugate within the contingencies of being. This identifies the signification of otherness, as though the antecedent to otherness toward the significance of necessary truth to the otherness of being. Where it concerns that this otherness is toward an existent that is a subject accordant with an otherness of being, it is that this is existence of otherness—where being is other to the existent that is other than being—is the antecedent that is toward another existent of an other being. This would be the other existent of being, that would have falsified its existence of being; for the otherness that was itself false within being. These as existents would be therein known as false beings, which would be for the purposes of what is purposive of being—*non-being*—that they were in effect the existents that were being of an otherness that was not in being; other than what was being of the negation of otherness that was their being. These would be as though within the totality that was the destruction of being as otherness. That this was its being as otherness, it was also its being as totality, where was considered a total being that would be known of an otherness that was within a totality *as* otherness;— shown as the presentation of a being that was the other to a being, as was known separate to the subject that was considered the being as in ownership. This being would be individuated to the being that was other to its *ownness*[32]—a responsible being of ownership.

[32] Husserl, Edmund, *Cartesian Meditations,(1960), Martinus Nijhoffe.*

Chapter 3 Idealism, Technology and Existential Phenomenology

The being within substance that is identical to the conditions as set forward by the principle of sufficient Reason, [33] is a conditional totality of the attributes of being as concurrent within substance of synthetic unity. The temporality of being is universalized contiguous with the conception of its object that is an instrument of thought. The instrument itself is the being-in-itself, outside of itself and within substance, now relational to the properties of a subject temporalized within the conception of the object as it relates to what is contemporaneous of its conditions from what has been representationed through the *principle of universal information.* [34]

The consciousness that is promulgated of itself, through the principle is in connection to the generality of the subject,—as in connection with the universality of consciousness that is in-itself the collectivity of attributes in connection with a particular value that relates to the temporal generality of an object that has been synthesized of conceptions, into an object that is now a technologically conscious being. Where in principle the being that is conjoined within the forms of representational media would there merge consciousness with technology, has synthesized a universal object that is technological of its being through this principle—it acknowledges the principle in connection with "tech-genera" that is the synthesis of object into a universally technological object that is in representation of the capacity for tech-genera through universal being; then furthered toward this an ontological manifestation of a technologized consciousness that has

[33] Schopenhauer's concept that representations in the world may be necessarily identified upon the threshold of a human understanding. Ibid., p. 7.

[34] This posits a concept that concedes particularity to a logic that is centered upon the notion that in the information age, data is more ontologically accessible where a particular subject is subsumed within its universal—subordinated by it, and reflexive of *de facto* representations and their propositional significations.

only to become independently pro-generative of genus to constitute its appearance as an existent that is in representation of genera proper. The object that is now in representation of both the temporal synthesis of being through the principle of universal information—as it is in representation of a technological being—is temporally infinite of its conditions that its synthesis has become contemporaneous with it as an existent. It follows from this that the synthesis of the technological being (in its contemporaneity) to a temporal being of infinite conditions, makes it contingent in relation to this infinite temporal being, of its conditions that are perceptually conditional to the subject, yet universal of its informational ideation. This universal ideation is the substrate to the object of its notion that it may be conceived, and in relation to the infinite temporal being that is its pro-generative impetus.

There the apprehension of the "technological object", is particular to the subject, that the attributes of the subject are in representation of the object as it appears within substance; with the principle of universal information as an informational substrate that refers to the qualities that are schematized of consciousness forming a subject, then those are posited in assignation as in relation to the subject as quantities that refer to an object on its notion. Formed of the initial representation that initiated the synthesis, the technological object of its synthesis is now in representation of the qualities that referred to the notion as it was initially relational to the informational contemporaneity that schematized consciousness of the Notionality as was then dynamical to the universal representation.

The synthesis of representational being that yields this informational technological being in representation of the infinite temporal being, now enters the collective will of consciousness as it is contemporaneously apprehended within a cultural plurality. This precipitates a decay to the temporal object's synthesis, as it breaks down from its direct relation as identical to its own particular being as existent of "tech-genera". As the object decays of its synthesis, it now becomes an object that is dynamically (as in a state of nature) relational to the collective will of the synthetic object, as it was apprehended from its synthesis as an existent. The informational substrate that referred the initial conditions of qualities in a subject to the collectivity relative to the representation of its collectivity of qualities,—schematizing consciousness of the principle of universal information, puts the technological being (that is an absolute) into a relativist collectivity that is before the principle of universal information. It follows now that the qualities in this relativity are contiguous to the synthetic technological object that is synthetically predicable of the relative qualities within the collective will as it stands in relation to its synthesis as an infinite temporal being. Though for all intents and purposes this "infinite temporal being" is referentially and representationally finite—the mathematical positing of Kant's infinite series of conditions, renders its finitude a radical impossibility, simply on the basis that the ontological proportions which form its progression through time, concerns infinity as an abstraction of an ever-expanding universe, reflexively entwined with humanity's conception of a Self as we stand in finite relation to the former.

A Phenomenological Historicity

Absolutes are what is in conception of a point in history that is its conditions as known, that these are identifiable of the contemporary knowledge that adheres to the significance of a specified period in history. The magnitude of awareness that is significant to this prescribed date, is the course of events in their conditions that have transpired, subsequent to the official date of an occurrence at a point in history. This is also representative of the cultures that existed throughout the periodicity of epochs that were in thought of a consciousness that conceived of its contemporary relevance so much,—that it carefully documented what was a morphological symbology; that would garner the inheritance of attachments that were the content present within historical facts as documented. This posits as an awareness, the historicity of an event, that is of its conditions, known from the facticity of the occurrence, then further known of a consciousness that is incurrent of the knowledge as present contingent with the description of events. That those same conditions do reappear in the natural course of history, it is of objective diachrony;—where the events of the past are repeated in a similar set of concurrent events, that are modified of a temporality. Such that the dynamical temporal associations are of synchronicity from a conditioned to the degree that the magnitude of historicity may reveal an event that had occurrence in the past, the temporal conditions were ripened of a critical mass of historical events in a present that fastened a conceptual reoccurrence of the event. The eschatological evaluation is one that proposes an identification of *epiphanical* phenomena—though for this the consideration that identifies a magnitude of historicity is evidenced, where the conditioned has from its finitude an indication of a contemporary occurrence that is corroborative to the synchrony of the present. A similar argument, that pursues knowledge of an ancestry through an ontology, reveals that the contemporary presence of phenomena are of their determinateness, the initial revelation toward what might in effect be an assignment of a determinateness to a relation that is in presence before its historical signification. That a determinateness is in appearance with an objective relation, it is in finite representation an *objectness*, yet terminable in its conditions as otherness. That a determinateness in its relationhood is representative of a property in its proximity that is indicated in the form of time experientially of its appearance, it is that this property is in appearance from an object that is finite in appearance:—that is its determinateness of a conditional otherness from an finitude of a priori conditions that are properties. Now that these properties are in finite representation of an otherness in its determinateness, and yet within infinite conditions that may be known a priori with conceptions, the properties themselves are predicable of a finitude that is the temporal totality of being of these as qualities of being. This engenders the pursuit of a complete being to the attainment of what is within phenomena, the necessary conditions of what will be known in the conception of a being other than the Self, that is an ancestor or predecessor—in that their conditions are finite in representation of infinite conditions that are within Genus the infinitude of properties as qualities of being.

Conditionality

Things in the world that are finite in representation, are *infinite* of their conditions. That they progress toward the *Unconditioned*, they can only be in an infinite *regressus* of those conditions that remain finite in representation as the very conditions in an infinite *progressus*. What are posited from conditions—both from propositions as from judgments that are contemporaneous with the temporal conditions—are in association with the finite representations that are presented in both a progressus of the conditions infinite in representation; as in an infinite *regressus* that is the contemporaneity of the contingency as conditions of being that are within this regressus inverted to the subject (of the object) that is the finite point of a contingency. The synchronic representations are as within actualities the contingent contemporalities to the conditionality of concurrent conditions from *progressus*—that are no longer contingent to the subject, but as actualities contemporary with the representations and conditions.

The conditionality that is of its conditions also of contingency—where the conditions are in their finitude themselves contingent to the conditionality of the subject, other than the contingency that is of the conditions in abstraction that are contemporaneously contingent to the subject—is of these contingencies, the conditionality of the conditions in abstraction that may have these contingencies that are finite in representation, but never as infinite conditions; only the contingencies that are contemporaneous with the subject are infinite to the conditions toward infinity, that are also these finite to the subject, though the contingencies are not known as parallel contingencies to the conditionality of the infinite conditions toward the unconditioned in their finite representation;—they are as this the *unconditioned.*

There are two main types of Contingencies

A Contemporaneous Object Contingencies B Conditional Contingencies

Of these there are four basic classes:

I actual II relational III phenomenal IV technological

Conditional contingencies are based on conditionality in abstraction, or contingent to the logical progressus of conditions from an actuality of its conditionality.

Actual Conditional Contingencies as Force in Magnitude

The conditions as they are infinite in progressus toward the unconditioned are then "as" contingencies to the subject from a previous conditionality—these are then as actual conditional contingencies in infinite *regressus* of the contemporaneous object contingencies. These are known of conditionality from their conception of their action as magnitudes that are the totality of things-in-themselves from the former conditionality to the present of conditionality in a relational abstraction that is force in magnitude.[35]

When infinite contingencies that are in representation of what is contingent to the conditions that are infinite to the conditionality of the subject in contemporaneity are in conception, it is that only in representation are they now in a *regressus* to the conditions of a previous contemporaneity—that is its conditionality. This indicates that the infinite conditions of a previous conditionality may identify the contemporaneous contingencies in *progressus*—that it has been apprehended from possibility as in a contingent conditionality.

This proposes a solution to the infinite regressus from a previous conditionality, that is in *progressus* of an actuality to a conditionality in its finitude, rather than in acknowledgement of a conditionality that is in presence of the Other through contingencies of being. This also posits the previous conditionality along with the contingency that it is now relational, and no longer in regressus of conditions relational to the

[35] The essential blending of Hegel and Schopenhauer here, must be utilized judiciously. The subjective will in-itself differs between philosophers. For the former, the will appropriates a subjective sensibility, and for the latter the will is an entry into the consciousness of the Other through its phenomenon. That an abstraction would yield a totalization of the being-in-itself is to be radically renounced as a possibility to the *Being* of Objectivity.

conditionality that is *in abstracto* of a contingency of being that is of an abstracted conditionality from the progressus of a contemporaneous conditionality contingent to the abstracted contingency.

When a thing is in progressus from a previous conditionality, and is contemporaneous in conception as a contingency, it is always truth. When thingness is contemporary of a contingency in its actuality—as conditions in abstracto that are contemporary of sensation—it is truth that the sensation is realized from conception of its conditionality and is contemporaneous to the will.[36]

A contingency is never truth unless it is contemporaneous with the image-in-representation that is its phenomena; a phenomenal contemporaneous object contingency, or a relational conditional "contemporary" contingency that is in abstraction concurrent with an image-in-representation that is infinitely in representation of a given situational object—which is not of truth, but is in finite representation of a previous conditionality to its situation that is now contemporary and in infinite *regressus* from the finite conditionality of a subjective Notionality.

The Notionality is then infinitely in representation of the object in a conditionality in finite regressus of a notion; that is now a conditional contingency in infinite representation, as well as it is a relational contemporaneous object contingency, in infinite regressus of a *nationality*—that is ever contiguous from technological contingencies to the conditions at conditionality *in abstracto*—that they are disclosed to the contemporaneous object contingency as in this *regressus* from the previous situationality of the subject's notion in abstraction.

The *in abstracto* situationality is then from its previous conditionality in infinite representation—yet never of those conditions infinite—that they are now contingent to the subject of the contemporaneous object contingency from the source that is its conditional contingency of the law that conditions are infinitely in a (logical) progressus toward the *Unconditioned.*

---

[36] Note here a variability in the *struggle* between Schopenhauer and Hegel—both contingencies to their own subjectivities, constituted by Kantian conditionality. Ibid., p. 20. The idea that an abstraction to the former gives subjectivity an instantiated "situationality" to the representational Other in *regressus*; while the latter is particular to its own universalization through an instantiation of a "contemporaneous object" constitutive to *Being*.

A contemporaneous object is actual to the conditionality of the contingent being—which is its representation that is infinite—and the contemporaneity of the object that is its in-itself of conduct, and contingent to the conditionality of the being of its conditions in infinite representation. Now the being that is contingent and in-itself, is no longer infinite, but contingent of its previous conditionality to the infinite representation that is in infinite regressus of the contingency of conditionality to the subject,—where the contemporaneity has become contingent.

This infinite representation is now the situational object of a previous conditionality of its conditions. These that are conditions *only* as image-representations that are abstracted of the subject from their own relationality from a precious conditionality, yet are the a priori positing of conditional attributes in the present conditionality that are then also in infinite regressus of the previous object conditionality.

That these are as aspects of the concurrent present conditionality, they are in regressus of their aspect truth at conditionality of the present—which is then not in infinite representation of the present conditionality—and is replaced by the infinite representationality of the image-in-representation from a former conditionality.

Representationality

Representationality is the contingent infinity of a former conditionality that is of each contingency, the situational object from a contingency,—that is in its relationality always expressed as the representational being in infinite regressus of the present conditionality; that is now contemporaneous with the conditions of a former conditionality. This signifies that conditionality is in regressus *a priori* to the previous conditionality then known as contingent, which is a contemporaneous object contingency to this subject in the present, then conditional to the subject in the former conditionality;—from this the a priori regressus acts as antecedent to the original conditionality that is its being contingent;

from here it is that the present conditionality is augmentative of its contingency that is *in abstracto* of the apprehension of the object contingency from the previous conditionality.

That the representation is of a thing, of its qualities, it is not the thing-in-itself, it is the conditionality of a representational object such as it is in its current state. The thing in-itself is the temporality of a thing, such that its totality is known infinitely at any point in time to be the same representational thing in a different state or of a different aspect; that its aspect is the partial conditionality of a thing where it has been absorbed of a contemporaneous property, and is only available in this aspect such that it has undergone a change and is so represented. (i.e. the burning of wood). This indicates that the infinite representation of a thing has also been moved in its actuality to another representational object in its former aspect of its state; and is there also contingent to the future conditionality of another thing, (i.e., the fire has spread).

An image-in-representation presents to us certain properties of matter, i.e., colour, form, relative size, speculative temporal actuality, environmental spatialization, proximal motion, etc., as it is contingent as a situational image-object while in appearance or signification of a totalized spatially-represented essence. This posits that the properties of matter are enacted from their ontological localization from thought—the kinesthetic actuality of the motion of properties—not the actual motion of the thing itself. Things themselves are never in motion of their properties as things-in-themselves, when within relative motion to other objects from force, so it is that representationality is the state where images-in-representation and representational objects, are in the state of flux that identifies the properties of matter, proximal to the thing-itself or its phenomenon—though never in consideration of the representation and the object in presence of dissimilar properties. The representational object is also a substrate to contingencies and other representational beings, such that these properties are now contingent to the proximities of those objects from motion of their phenomena—then in a furtherance of thought toward the object in presence, where relative motion is coincident with the properties of matter. This object of its motion, is then only animated from force, where its momentum is in conception of this movement. As the representational object is made an image-in-representation within mind, it is with this that the properties of matter-in-motion of this in principle, are what the thing-itself is of its matter—as properties also to be considered substance. Through this, it is only that the things themselves will be known of substance, that is also in appearance of the images-in-representation of the unconditioned;—that here a finitude of conditionality, is posited of its contemporary conditions, and in actuality founded contemporaneously with the phenomena that is of its properties, a being in-itself. This image-in-representation is the signification of a positing of substance to the being in question.

This representation is finite to the properties of matter that are variable to motion. So it is that the contemporaneous temporality, is perceptual of a horizon that acts within the immanence of a substance that is within its representation, conditional to an infinite variability concerning its action. The same horizon of its representational characteristics, is preserved within motion as the properties of matter, toward finite temporal abstractions. As *existents* from which a representation is within the concurrent contemporalities, those are contemporaneous to the contingencies found from infinite systems, yet the horizon of an object in representation is an image-sign posited or moved, so as to signify its movability—that its action is in representation of those conditions as held within the properties of matter and the positing of substance. This condition is understood within an antecedence at interiority. This without its reification, is a conditionality that is infinite where concerns its contemporaneity;—the relational characteristics must correspond with the representational object in its conditionality, in so far as would be experience, the representational properties of matter in a conditionality that were moved in opposition to its *permanence of substance*[37], with a representational object in object-substance unity. This unity does not correspond with an image-in-representation outside of its medium through form.

The object is also in its *aspect* color, which is the temporality of a thing itself, where the motion is timed separately from other objects of differing colors (the differentia), and similarly to objects of dissimilar colors. The combination of all colors in the spectrum is clearly the fastest motion of light. This presupposes that a change has occurred in the object with respect to its color, necessitating the conclusion that the motion of a thing in-itself, toward another thing in-itself, is always articulated through its absolute of motion where color is present in the image. That color is

---

[37] Ibid., p. 20.

present in all objects themselves, it is that they are therefore in motion constantly. It must follow then that our sense is responsible for the interpretation of what is perceived as having its coherence based in the state of motion, more than in its stasis. That is its essential momentum where representations are no longer prone to the force of magnitude, and are relational of force from relative acceleration to other things themselves; even further that the elements are known as things that they present color that will undergo changeables[38] to another temporality. The motion of color defines a significance of what is movable of objects from their changeables—of their own temporality that is its matter component. Though mass is the relative stasis of an object to its relative mass within force from acceleration, the object magnitude is of this quotient, within its stasis as changeables are articulated by color. Though this would appear false, it is essential to discover the representationality of an object where concerns color, in contrast to one that is not of color through its representational aspects.

If all matter were considered to be in a constant state of flux as Heraclitus had, then it would mean that the use of matter in its aspect would be presented both by its purpose (tools); but also by its essential quality that was of another use to us that interacted with matter in such aspects that its role as matter in flux was in presence of different (aspect) changeables to the other object. Where it is a combination of a thing that is of use to us, and one that is elemental to nature (a House and the rain), it is that the house is perceived of its representation to fulfill our needs of shelter, and that the rain is something effectual of a causation that will potentially get us wet,—but that the effectual perceived purpose of each are in relation, such that the purpose of each is satisfied within each of their aspects. Should the house begin to leak water, the rain has then become effectual to a change in the basic quality of the house, that is now affected by the same cause as is the rain showers themselves. The important conclusion is that the rain is in motion of its effects from cause, and is in representation of effects toward another representation that is in its construction purposive of its effects;—though in its actuality only in

---

[38] Aristotle's *Metaphysics*(346 BC.) The concept that the object of thought—that also represents an attribute to a subject as a property of substance (ousia, eidos, etc.)—may be moved, changed or modulated by Others to which they stand in representation (relation) and as others stand in relation to subjectivity (self-identity).

representation of those effects, that are now also effectual to other effects from other causes. The significant thing to observe here, is that only from motion do we recognize the change in the basic quality of the house where it leaks. From reason, it is that now the purposiveness of the representation is enacted of an effect from nature, that is its representation now also purposive of its effects; with laws of motion forming the experienced change in the representations of their purposiveness to another "dynamical" plateau. From this it is certain that we may ascertain that motion and purposiveness, having designated the matter that is in representation of its flux, as now collapsed to a state that is known of a change in purposiveness from effects; the things-in-themselves are known of this change.

Collectivity

I The collective authority of an individuated principle through technology in representation of a collective—that is markedly in appearance on its horizon as a possibility in contingency, yet also as an actual contingent to the general conditionalities—is an indebtedness.

II A general assembly that is unified in conception from a possibility that is the "forum" of thought that presents individual beings-in-themselves through a technological representation that is its machine is a generality. The idea of inter-connectedness is found in presence of the machine, and is the form of content within all aspects of the consideration of what is content.

The collectivity is itself—the infinite conditions of a technological infinity—as is within its conception the generality of what is a prerequisite to the generality. The collectivity is based on a representational synthesis of concurrent requisites that are then assembled into a singular purpose—through the agreement with the conditions of the generality in its general contingent requirement in place of a contingency of being. The contingent being is then replaced with the available being as within its compliance, no longer contingent of the conditions of being before a collective; but in accordance with those the very same as an *a priori* necessity of the collective. This is realized in convention, the abstraction of necessary being in accordance with a collectivity of its collective properties, that are no longer in contrast to the properties in appearance of the contingency of being, and contingent to being in contingency; with technological representations that are both within the provisions of media as they are within the machinery configured from culture such as it is.

The media culture weaponry arms the collectivity of its generality, with corporatist phenomenal magnitudes that are before and in relation to the properties in question of the nature of appearances, and with respect to properties that are the judgments that administrate the contemporaneous ethical dynamics in the availability of qualities.

Now that the substratum of the Self is contemporaneous with the inter-connectedness of things through the media culture, and of its technological representations and machinery, it is always that being is contingent to these contemporary devices of the culture—just as it is that they present the self with a contingent being. This contingent being is however, always in representation of existing conditional truth in its relationality.(i.e.., the content in a television program is dynamically represented in a proximal relation in content representation). As these qualities of the self are now in representation of cultural instruments of the media such as are these, it is that the proximity of properties is always in contingency with the contemporaneity of substratum of the self, along with the substrate that is its media inter-connectedness as it corresponds with action.

The nuclear thought during cultural reifications in representation of an existing content.

This is an in-itself of causality that has for it no representations in the world, and where it is contemporaneous with an existent that may be effectual of its conception. This conception is not from a Kantian object of experience, but from an analytical judgment that resolves to a conditionality and posits its conception within a cause of its conditions.

Rational Empiricism

A rational empiricism that has its practice within facticity, posits the conception of its conditions in any situation *a priori*. In order to practice facticity with things-in-themselves, it is necessary to abstract the facticity of a situational conditionality that it is in relation to its conditionality through an a priori conception. A magnitude of facticity that is its probe, is available to search proximity of the will with a priori conceptions; though it is also probable that beings-in-themselves already with this magnitude in conception of a subject, may deceive a subject of its notion with the incorrect information. The rational empiricism that defeats this potentiality, is in conception of a subject of its conditions, and simply posits the situational condition and discloses its proximity of the thing-in-itself, as an indicator of the truth of proximity to a being, in advance of its empirical conditionality in greater detail. Where things are in situation of a conception they will appear in relation to the magnitude that is of beings-in-themselves, in relation to a magnitude that is the facticity *of* beings themselves.[39]

Corporatist Phenomenal Magnitudes

The corporatist phenomenal magnitudes and public generalities are known as component entities that represent individuated action within the middle term that can be of neither. This action is contemporary within the requirements of a corporate manifold that is instrumental to the maintenance of a media system. As a relational systemization of media ideologies, it is the beneficial implementation of concurrent mass-

[39] One can here perceive the close filiation between the work of Kant *via* Schopenhauer, in an existential twist of fate with Sartre's authentic Genus inside Husserl's noetic stratification of a Self. Where this identifies with the Hegelian project, it is noted that the Object of thought—in its Quantum state (*The Science of Logic*, 1816)—there is no concept to being-qua-being, other than its mediation through the Other.

conditioning that places public contingents in agreement with corporate programming. This hegemonizes activities in the middle term, such that reflection in coalescence with media forms, is annexed into those contemporary requirements as are found within contingent systems; that have now been made actual in a “campaign” that is the terminal point of conditionality; such that the conditionality in relationhood to a contingency of being of media systems, has been mobilized of relations in pursuit of the Notionality of the contingencies themselves. This is what we will now identify as an actualization of relational contingency at interiority, in an appropriation of the corporate body. This actual conditional appropriation is of a governmental instrumentation that “valorizes” the content of a notion to a system of public Notionality, then augmenting this public Notionality of its generality, through particular relational corporate conditionalities, so as to posit its notion in substance from the collectivity of conditionalities as articulated through media consent. This articulates its paroxysm in the middle term, where media conditionality is non-coalescent with anything ideological that is governmental in a public sense, that instrumentalizes consciousness of iconoclastic representations, where all judgments fail of these paradigms, and are then made contemporary with similar conditionalities through the generality of the principle of universal information.[40]

An Argument for Transcendental Idealism

The manifold identical is in a multiplicity of collective consciousness as a collective identical of truth-in-itself. This is contingent of both economic strata as it is intersubjective of a transcendental ideal. This inherent contradiction between transcendence and economic strata of any supervenience over the sense-components of substance, is a profound problem to the contemporary administration of any ethic whatsoever. The great revelation is that the transcendental idealism has been overrun with the determinateness of a pure materialism which is the soul perceptual knowledge to the notion of value where concerns an actuality. Of truth, it

---

[40] Ibid., pp. 69-70.

is that the synthetic proposition has become an end terminal point for apodicity that operates under the guidance of an economic setting that principles its ethics of a *materialiter*[41] actuality.

This is a great source of danger to the "contemporarian" that is acting in accordance with an actuality that is predominantly of proximity to a subject, based on its formative experience in universal substance of its particularity—that a being has fortressed its life force in a more historical sense where concerns its manifold attributes that are incurrent of the very act of being; just as they are predicable of universal substance where concerns the accrued state of proximal qualities to a subject, that are then issued into a transcendence of the pure understanding. This confers with the truth that an object has for its understanding a being that is not in-itself material, but extended into a phenomenal horizon that gives permanence to its attributes of certain infinite conditions. This permanence is yet never realized of the apodictic concretion of self (ego sum) of things-in-themselves, built in concretion of an essence of the collective identical materialiter, but is necessarily in conquest of this where remains the ethical contradiction of transcendence to apodictic concretions of self to the collective identical. These self-constituting essences are also undergoing determinations where concern the manifold properties of substance, and are as things-in-themselves known of their socio-physical properties as objects of every geo-science that has economized these very objects into any quantifiable entities. The rational proportions of this science, depends most on the economic categorical imperative of the intersubjective object, and depends least on the outcome of the subject in relation to the object under-going such determinations, as are manifold to the same monad as is constituted of the subject *originaliter*. [42] For this, it is that the subject's ongoing determinations must be reconciled in the immediacy of a proposition based of a materialism, in representation of things themselves as would designate the absolute ego of the subject as constitutive of material considerations *only*—that for these reasons there were no other means by which to constitute the subject commensurably.

---

[41] Kant's *Metaphysics of Morals* (1797)—refers to ontological substances as they exist in material form, and are thereby reified by certain natural, private, public, provisional, and (divine) rights.

[42] Ibid., p. 68.—refers to the positing of certitude that original matter composes human reality from a subjective source as a "psychophysical being" constituted by and through a community of monadic egos.

The short fall of this is that the subject's ongoing determinations of their transcendence in the apodicity in verification thereof, are resolving to things-in-themselves, rather than separate determinations of the self that exist within and throughout a universal substratum that has for it a temporality extending toward infinity. This nullifies the infinite conditions of substance in the determinations of an ownness-essence—thusly suggesting that the transcendence of being toward an idealism had met with its untimely demise as it had become in the collectivity of *distributiva communitiva*, [43] before it has appeared in representation to a subject as proximal cause to the understanding; something that does terminate the idealism that otherwise would be transcendent of a subject.

It is however more than likely that this circumstance is made commensurate to the civil condition on the basis that it has been rendered of possibility, but never of any limitations within anything coercive of manifold properties constitutive of a subject—these that are also necessary in the act of commensuration toward the satisfaction of an obligation toward a duty. It is under such circumstances that it is only ethical under the civil constitution for the subject to constitute a self while under *lex permissiva*, [44] whereby it is duly noted that no such coercive limitations will hinder a subject from the very act of the concretion of self of its own-essential determinations toward the fulfillment of such as would be any duties applicable to the concretion of self, of its determinateness toward a more transcendent idealism. It is thereby in proposition that what we are concerned with an ethical transformation, that is in effect more of a medical contradiction where concerns the necessary supervenience of a life force of its own actuality, before a materialiter collective identical with intersubjective manifold determinations. This threat puts the notion of essence under more scrutiny of the categorical imperative, as it superposes the requirement of a constitution such as the transcendental constitution of the objective world—this which puts object-identicals monadically in association with manifold properties that must have for them a historical horizon to supersede. This proposes that there must be an infinite *progressus* of conditions that form a phenomenal representation of

---

43 Ibid.,p.84. As such, the community must benefit from the same rights universally as its members.

44 Ibid., pp.84-85. Whereto the permissions extended to a subject are within the pursuit of their own life's interests, they must be in accordance with a duty that is its law.

the monadically objective world, to consider any degree of inter-subjectivity of the additionally compulsory rational horizon. These two horizons present both a transcendence of possibilities, within a historical context to the individual, just as they satisfy the need for a contemporary dialectic. Such as would be primarily represented monadically, and of the objective world, it is that with these horizons in a constitutive synthesis that the subject never undergoes such intersubjectivity as would be of any anguish, yet is represented within the context of collective being that has for its own reflection truth-in-itself, and has for its intersubjectivity an objective world in representation of the commensurate determinations of a subject contingent to rational-historical manifold determinations, that are infinite in progressus to the unconditioned; yet known of such determinate conditions as do appertain to the subject in verification of its own manifold being.[45] These would be essential to the secure constitution of an ownness-essence under such conditions for the transcendental ego in the process of identification of an object that has for it in representation, the synthetic proposition that opposes the subject of its own determinateness; such as would not only limit the subject in constitutive synthesis, but would also coerce the community out of any such determinations whatsoever—which would present quite an obvious antinomy to the naked eye where concerns the constitutive self. That these very determinations are in the constitutive synthesis of the subject in its determinateness, it is also that of its distribution it has so to constitute the availability of its own determinations in connection with a community of things-in-themselves,—moreover to consummate the actualities and potentialities of the collective identical. Yet if these manifold properties are so in distribution of the subject in its own determinateness, it is that such actualities—as are constitutive of the subject *originaliter*—must undergo certain a priori determinations that are evidenced throughout the apodictic concretions of self. The subject has for its own-essentialness an intersubjectivity that proposes an objective world that confers with an immutable concretion of the self, to commensurate the extremely barbarous lack of verification that any transcendence had occurred; a

---

[45] This insofar as manifold being is particular to Leibniz's monad, and therewith accompanied by a logic that had identified the *unconditioned* of Kant, as this which would propel contingencies posited from collective determinations toward horizons where intersubjective reasoning were made possible in spite of Schopenhauer's *principium individuationes*. Ibid., p 7.

moment that would ensure the subject that its proximate cause were under the attack of an arch enemy or vicious criminal. The constitutive essence of the subject is without question under such coercion as in an act of wrong-doing, when things-in-themselves have for them an opposition, that has for its synthetic proposition the proposition of illness, or the forceful administration of an economic imperative. This occurs in a manifold mode of givenness and has for its inherent dynamical composition, a collectivity of objects that undergo only such determinations as are within the propositions of the intersubjective object itself—no doubt an object that is practicing its own ethical contradictions.

The transcendence of being of an idealism has for it a representation of a supra-temporal collective consciousness of beings themselves, though not in-themselves, and of noetic strata of the ecstatical[46] horizon that appertains to the conception of conditions under considerations of a subject. It should be referred to as the ecstatical transcendence of being, that any of the manifold properties of a subject are of their infinity of conditions, as represented to a collective of beings in a synthesis that constitutes those manifold conditions.

This presupposes the existence of a singular horizon that exists for a subject of its own transcendence, where it reflects a sense-constitution to the conditions of a subject as they are at the point of *ecstasis* felicitous of being, as of being toward a transcendence; this supports the all embracing a priori of Husserl, that subjects are under such conditions as are constitutive of the self to a collective that is thereby so represented of the objective world to a particularization of self that undergoes its own determinations without any intersubjectivity whatsoever.

The collective identical

The manifold identical stands in relation to universal substance *a priori* as a function of the constitution of self of any individual. When a collective engages the individual, in connection with the perception of the manifold identical as a set of objects within substance, it is conceivable that the

[46] Heidegger, Martin, *Being and Time* (1927). The essential idea that Dasein (being-in-the-world) has for it a transcendental horizon that is particular to the existential phenomenology of subjectivity, while monitored through *care* and a *readiness-to-hand* (givenness).

representation of the significant object relation, is in form of the collective identical. This means that the subject is represented at the manifold level to vast collectives, while in conception of an object that then becomes the object so represented collectively of its own identical. This signifies an object that is thereby undergoing its own determinations before the objective world in conception of its own manifold object, that is the otherness of the identical. While in perception of this object, the subjective object undergoing its determinations is collectivized in connection with its manifold object, that then represents this that is now a subject to another subject of the collective identical. Effectively it is reproduced throughout the collective *a priori* when the perceiving subject has for it a manifold identical that is in representation to a collective a priori and of the will. This formulates the a priori constitution of the subject where concerns their own manifold being, and subsequently confirms and makes verification that the subject is undergoing its own determinations in relation to other subjects in circulation of the manifold identical *a priori*—confirming the maxim as formal law that the determinateness of the apodictic totality in a living being is valid a priori. This solves many problems where concerns intentionality, as now the only object of inter-subjective intentionality is its object-in-connection—the object relation. It is considerably more likely to enjoy phenomenal inter-actions with this being the case than by way of genetic intentionalities[47] clashing within substance of the manifold identical, which contains properties that are required, desired, or willed by either subject-object. It is under these circumstances that we encounter the innate character of the brute to be the intrinsic inheritor where the subject has fallen of its own facticity below to the primordial substratum out of its upper noetic strata that gave it any such manifold being to begin with. For this it is that the ethical incentive is a source of falling for *Dasein*, [48] and that in turn it stands to lower the beings that are ascendant of any primordial stratification of substance and well-constituted of its manifold being; whether or not they are in current possession of the manifold properties as represented to them of the manifold identical. This only begins to deconstruct social Darwinism, as it

[47] Husserl's concept that the ego cogito of its *ownness* essence is posited aiming toward its own objects, and also such objects other than its own.

[48] In the most literal Hegelian and Heideggerian sense possible, I am referring to *a being-in-the-world* as disclosed as both subject to objectivation by the Self and the Other in its own disclosedness.

assures the strong of their own survival, while jeopardizing the fates of the weaker. It would seem that constitutive a priori noetic strata—manifold of being to the extent that it is intersubjectively represented of the collective identical—suggest that it is more than likely we are able to live independently of our represented constitutive selves; that in effect the causality of our being is self-perpetuating of its manifold identical with a priori determinations that inter-relate to subjects, and are forming the necessary proximate causality so as to constitute the collective identical. This is an ordinance of self that suggests that it is possible to build the phenomenal substrate above primordial being once and for all, and to assure that our human evolution does in fact take place outside of any contradictions that jeopardize the future of the species. This is an argument for a genus that begins to rule our sense perception, for the knowledge of perception is a living solution to healthier corporeal systems. The eternal soul will have more luck with sense perception once it is independent of the ramifications of having sense experiences that involve sensation—primordial knowledge that recognizes any act of privation as a direct assault on a sensibility. This occasion is a question of the proximity of substance where concerns the action of a subject-object toward another subject-object that stands before a needed attribute, and leaves the first subject-object no other choice put to employ privation as a means of acquisition of the attribute so as to perform a duty or task. It is that when this duty or task does involve the civil condition, that it becomes more socialized of the public sense of currency, where it is more likely that a facticity falling or the falling of *Dasein* will incur primordial damage to the subject, rather than the rubber glove effect of a privation that is known of sensation without a facticity falling;—one that in fact sustains none of the same damage as does the privation that takes place at the primordial level. For these considerations we will refer to that plateau of consciousness that is purely noetic in contrast to the level of consciousness that is strictly primordial as the political-economic substrate.[49]

---

[49] This in a sense is referring to Husserl's noetic stratum, which is a vertical ontological instantiation to representational consciousness, while identifying with Gilles Deleuze in the sense of the *plateau*—whilst tarrying away with a Marxist notion of primordial humanity as the agents of the ontological stratum existing in both of those expressions of the subjective pole.

As much as philosophy would wish to avoid political considerations to the extreme, it is on this one occasion that we find the substrate to be administrable of communities more than of a direct form of government maintenance. So we find that the reciprocity of any government system is being realized by way of a relationship, whereby the public carries out the mandate based on their own personal experience with government, and that there is no direct involvement at this stage that preserves anything other than the technological socio-cultural forms that define the collective state of the media consciousness of any given sociological region. For this it is that the substratum itself is formed representationally by the population and media systems, and of any material actuality by all forms of active government.

We see here that there is a fundamental problem in terms of any constitution whatsoever, as there must be in preservation of the constitutional monarchy itself, presence in appearance of the monarch, just as there is presence of the constitution by which the status of factual currency is presupposed as functional of any system of governance that involves the health imperatives of modernity in the technological age. Here we discover that with knowledge of the political-economic substratum, and proper relations with the concern for what is a constitutional monarchy, that the presence of the monarch outside of material currency will be an experience of reason—a noetic encounter that posits a consciousness of the monarch, identical in representation to millions—in preservation of the a priori constitution of subject-object determinateness where concerns their collectivity in constitution. This will become an actuality more necessary in preservation of healthy bodies, and healthy minds for the greater health of the populous. Very important questions come to mind that reflect on the status of any such thing as would be a body-politic where concerns this constitution of self within a collectivity that supervenes with economic concerns for the totality that *do* create this political-economic substrate. How do the lower classes survive when it is only disease that is upon them when put to the task of survival in the modern age? How do the rich reconcile their own collective constitutions when there is nothing constitutive to their being within the masses that are all wrapped up within the primordial essences of the bodies, that can and will strip way essence from the more economically fortunate without a proper constitutive bridge between primordial essence and noetic strata?(not primordial being(nor here suggested to be of the brutes)). It is here suggested that the primordial essence of any being is constituted without any inter-relation that consummates the a priori presence of a manifold identical in circulation of a subject-object to the degree that the political constitution of society must make it viable for any human artifice to sustain their equiprimordial[50] being within the culture—without the frequent attacks of those of the political-economic substratum—that have become lodged in battle over currency that puts them in context with the under-classed, yet raises the stakes much higher, such that the value of the under-classed then becomes their value; in effect their causal relations create a circumstance whereby the under-classed remain primordially under fire to support the upper-strata without any recompense whatsoever for their donations of constitutive self. Here again the political constitution is very much required to preserve those facets of the artifice's ability, such that they can be made more productive members of society. It is that we need to stop thinking that so many citizens must be put out and victimized to make the remainder of the citizenry happy:—that is the sum total of our conclusions to date where concerns the political constitution or any of its suspensions from region to region. Any nation state cannot sustain its whole population with these in consideration, while not acknowledging the necessity of relinquishment from the civil condition, where civil rights are being vanquished for corporate growth to enable the same parties as were within their own enablement to begin with—when the initial violation was taking place; as within despotic states. With constitutive truths known a priori, we may be on the road to salvaging the situation, and sorting through the wreckage to mount further potentialities that advance the culture beyond its media technocracy. This advancement would prove the collective health of the species when it no longer became necessary to employ the greatest evil on Earth—illness—and would sooner consummate our relationship with the ascendant superior species, that we are as we constitute equiprimordial machinery, far superior to that of any technological artifice. The technologizing of consciousness that reaches this apex in the collectivization of the identical-self provides a truthful solution to the early beginnings of our understanding as to how to overcome the ever-emergent problems

---

[50] Heidegger's term for the ontological stratum that is vertical to the existence of the primordial terrain (ground (German *Grund*)) on which being is posited as within the Self or out there in the world as a closed totality. Ibid., p.87.

throughout nature as we evolve through the technological age. That these would be forms which were known to us throughout perceptions in filiation with a logic that were represented by a world to which we had become accustomed as a posited totality accompanying the theoretical aspirations abstracted through cultural mediums, beyond the social transformation made possible by signified positions of global awareness, we must remain within an ontological field where the movements governing collective responsibilities continue to examine the existential phenomena with which to proceed, toward a horizon that we've conditioned both from the resources within our control; and from the positions that we are able to adopt in order to mobilize social change within the coordinates of events that exist to us as signified potentialities that are transcendent to the limiting properties that are posited by unconditioned actualities.

Chapter 4

Bio-Technological Transcendence

The natural order of humankind is something that some of us never would have expected to be situated within the ambit of a never-ending disavowal of our present political economy. What is real to those that operate from a condition of disrepair remains however, within the logic of a plan that possesses the soul of a country, while it completes its own identical source of reasoning where the night unfolds just as the day begins—starlight echoing throughout the coordinates where life examined existence without the necessary process of discovery, that society might yield from its horizon to the same experience that had become of an articulation of why nothing matters more, than the spirits of those that embodied collectives persevering through extensions of the self that are at the best of times, nothing less evident than the concept that we'll begin to fade to the same position where we had first become—always seeking the repairs of what would realize similar doubts on what had motivated us to strive from the onset of the problems to which we had succumbed.

Given the currency of what compels society's thoughts forward, through the troughs of political reality, into a thread of being that is inured with its prospects as a forward-moving machinery of self-generating principles that captured the hearts of so many, that we are prone to accept them as rational participants of a symbolic order of inner truth; we must peruse the depths of what drives ideas like those that are dictated by institutional powers with a vigour resonating upon the shores of where we had first encountered hopes of achieving the heights of *societal* becoming—beyond the passive encumbrances of a complacency to will as those acting as carriers of a wisdom that had never fully blossomed in former years to the same extent. That we had transferred the lessons of the past, as though it were simply a disordered or frenzied attempt to reconcile differences, completed by what had appeared from the wishes of dreams encompassing the representations cumulative of lost causes, and faded attempts to save the culture from its own vanities with a projection of the will of a creative ambition—greater than the world had ever conceived would have become realized within the days of its own inception.

As a culture of self-reflective species-beings, [51] that had endeavored to transcend future controls that accompanied our own utility, to the point where existence is the very engine that drives humanity forward through time—we cannot help but admit—where the promises of former generations have outlived most of our expectations, they have yet to supersede the transmission of its own short-fall to generations that are yet to arrive.

With this, we have the power of language as the first tool of what thrusts the energies compelling humans, beyond the stations where they are encountered within the residual artefacts of a failure to proceed, without first taking heed of the process that had natured the human spirit within its more well-conceived formation of a collective multiplicity of particular classes of well-organized, socially comprehensible, well-represented creatures, undivided within the quest for a return to a universal position of independence at the very source of humankind's explorations of the outermost reaches of the free societies where control once dominated the former. Also while transferring a composition to natural progress, that would beckon us toward a horizon where the concepts shaping our political and economic climate, are not necessarily independent of the aesthetic purposes that dialectically predispose humanity toward a discourse that galvanizes its own conscious terrain—partaking of the fruits of its own labours while reaching out, in order to transform reality as though it is a never-ending, ongoing project that will only see the light of day once we have departed the point where we had left our present for a horizon that were developed from a sound relationship to the past—without falling in to the same traps that had threatened us with an outcome unduly responsive to where we continued

[51] A term coined by Feuerbach that had been utilized to consider the substance of *being*, while identifying with an abstract potentiality of an appropriation of humanity, through an instinctual and natural relation to technologies (those both human and inhuman) that involved the social praxis of the object as it stands in relation to a totality of which it had been horizontally composed as distantiated from subjectivity.

to repeat the same errors, thinking that we are impervious to the disasters that have made us what we are today.

Given that the tomorrows are as the yesteryear of the never having yet occurred, certain structures which determined the visibility of what appears to us a more viable form, this of which constitutes a knowable object to humankind—the culture that defines the multiplicity of which endeavors are to be consumed in appropriate manners, through public availability—there is a radical sense of dissociation between subjectivity and the thing that most fascinates us. As we are creatures facilitated by quotidian practices, just as all those that had been before, and all whom are to follow, the concepts that drive our senses of pleasure—or the condemnation thereof—are repelled by the prospect that there may be something lurking in the shadows, behind the projection of this that had propelled manifestations of the image that we had formed of ourselves from an infancy of self-recognition; to the responses that we had begun to direct toward others as equal participants within the stratified conception of us as beings-in-themselves. Thereto, one would be remiss to suggest that the coordinates of a humanity that condones the appropriation of the other as an object of joy or fascination, would be to submit to a condition for which no patience in the realities that formed its representation within the mind as a contiguous substance, would be accepted within the realm of any notion of possibility. In order to satisfy the outer regions of this that determines self-reflexive conduct as an appropriation of the context that derives an excess of personal freedom away from its opposition upon horizons, where thoughts are only determinable of abstractions of the singular positions with which they are in filiation, nothing is more reasonable than what may posit an identical presupposition to the one that is instantiated by the hold that modern wisdom has upon the conceptual forms of transcendence—pushing beyond the barriers at the edge of where the essence of humanity is reified through traditions of accumulation, and projected into the stratospheres of bio-technology, [52] as a rarified and genetically presupposed condition of the chosen and identifiable species that are to have run of the planet in advance of a collective formalization of the

[52] Ontologically considered to have become manifest upon millennial horizons, as a position that projects possibilities for human transcendence that are beyond the expectations of prior generations as to the significance of technological developments (improvements)*sic*.

human resources that substantiated a natural impetus to develop potential—through an identical precondition of heightened social and political awareness of the inward gaze, afforded the energies of commonplace symbolic beings, ordered into positions where the abstractions possible of existential truth are more potent than the artificial means which allows for them to promulgate things identical to the ones from whence they had founded their origins.

It is without control, or a sense of highly motivated insight for freedom however, that the visibility of the conditions most viable to social progress would become more and more a part of accumulation in-itself; and less a particular symbolic component to the subject in exposition of which freedoms had been engaged through the process of a progressive accumulation of subjective emancipation, beyond the appropriation of subjectivity into a condition that had become more visible to an awareness that were prone to impose a condition that presupposed the viability of subservience to an invisible authoritative body-politic; governed *stricto sensu* by an extremely minute proportion of the more visible public—in which it had determined itself to be the ruling faction of the political enterprise *in toto*.

That totality is never to see the light of day on the face of planet Earth once again without first having adulterated its originary composition as a horizon of absolute productive control of social and political developments—beyond the individual wills of those for whom the appropriation of personal space, amounts to becoming a receptacle for appropriated levels of controlled and well-mannered speech during inane interactions. We will willfully condone the former, such that the subjective position as an enduring vital component of the symbolic invisibility of humanoid syntactical reason, is an verifiable ineffability toward a promulgation of symbolic space transcending its limitations; where the ontological representation had already failed to propose extensions of the individual Self that had been adequately and soundly represented to the stratifications of those of the outer most anointed regions of the symbolic unconscious[53]—and more presently to a symbolic reality that conjures self-identity, where it has been encumbered with the outer extensions of consciousness, in filiation with horizons where

[53] A concept derived from the Freudian *unconscious*, while paying heed to his late readings of Schopenhauer and the symbolic experiences that he had posited as functional to space, time, and causality, matter and form.

naturalized human endeavors encounter horizons, where individual perspectives would be subsumed to a universality that had been present within the logic of what had originated within the symbolic incarnations that had instantiated a transference of subject to world; in gestures manufactured by a representational potency that were presupposed through the generative composition of bio-technology, and the socio-political movements associated with human transcendence beneath the logic that undermines the promulgation of an intersection between symbolic reality and a more concrete formalization of the world as a universalized horizon of particular individualities.

Chapter 5 The Symbolic Dimension

Though as things may appear in-themselves to be never outlasting their position as a place of unadulterated fusion with the concepts, wherein they may originate as a particular species of ideas—these for which a conclusive appeal to the endeavors that shape a discourse as an operation that needs no other introduction than its subjugation of what eliminates its own possibility—we are infinitely irreducible to a proposition that sits where the dimensions of estimated public value consider the vision in which we have adumbrated conditions of exchange so as to accommodate a grandiose attempt to subordinate exclusivity *en-masse*.

Through the optics that perform a synthetic operation upon the attempts to project a more intensified sense of resolve to transcend those horizons, where only boundaries that are beyond our escape find equal footing with the coordination of administrable doubts, verifying subjects' poles of consciousness, as these which are particular to the Other, wherever it acts in accordance with a visibility originating in available content; such is the state for those that would have otherwise wished to subordinate visibility to the auspices of an endangerment that were situated within a coordination of affairs that transferred visibility, to transparent inclusions of self-identical truth that had already become part of the logic that had generated a public discourse, that had kept the victorious in power throughout a period where visibility had reached the level of totality for the public arts. Thereto concluding its appeals to the more private considerations of factions that had glimpsed upon the resolutions formed through an established discourse, found within most world nation-states that had not been appropriated by the same measures of time that annihilated effectual distributive justice, to the core of a reality where social decay were more readily situated upon the horizon than the predecessors to the movement had coordinated as measures to supply the public with a discourse that had sustained them within their own positions of power.

As a *de facto* reality that suspends an originary conduct that dissolves into a sustained and unbridled conclusive appeal to appearances that render public viability inane and unjust ever for mass-consumption—should this act in accordance with constitutional privilege in-itself—the embodiment of what society had envisioned as its necessary projection of authentic self-identity, has reached a horizon where visibility is limited by its magnitude in the inauthentic measures which have accommodated its position—as this which would represent an authenticated administrative body politic that had originated within the same emancipatory justice that had been presupposed within its instantiation as the administrative body, coordinated with a public's own emancipatory self-identification. [54] Where administrative justice fails a body politic, it does so with the universal within mind. Yet the souls of humankind depend upon universality as the correct measure of the particularities from which it were formed—in what had been synthetically constituted by those willing to project from their subjective position through the transformative components conditioned by discursive activities, and never the distractions of public programmes coordinated so as to dissuade discourse from its responsibility to become well-informed and represent the wills of those for whom a position of juridical authenticity is well-earned—within a durability that had never succumbed to shallow triumphs, and ill-mannered consumers of an emancipatory justice that would be fully willing to leave the troubadours and the mavericks alone; in place of deposing those for whom the fifth amendment had become more powerful in North-America than its home in the freedoms presupposed by the first one that had been conceived.

Moreover, that the symbolic momentum of what had driven cultural politics so steadily forward, had also thrown its signifying component into a state of disarray with the essence of this for which there had only been opinions that were to be consumed as a public resource in-itself. Where Being, as with existence—or the Heideggerian *existenz*—is symbolic to the moment where it first repairs the gaze, from where it had been instantiated as a glow upon a horizon, where the public condoned a disclosure that appropriated its position from its transcendence as a knowing thing that would appear to us in all of its splendour. Subsumed within the symbolic appearance of what is there to become of the glimpse that we possessed from a conscious absolute of the conceptual form that

---

[54] A post-structuralist, essentialist ideal, that posits being as its own formal identity as causal to the Self—as identical to itself; and identical to the Other once it has realized its own individuated existence from mediations to its own particularity.

is represented to us a living object—contingent to the determinations that are compelled by a subjective state of a supersession of forms by content—we become transparently entwined with representations that radiate an inward appeal to the display of aesthetic information; as though consciousness is more suitable as an inner truth most responsive to what the transcendence of content into the outer regions of thought would suggest. Here logic presumes its presence as a necessity of the forms themselves that are inherent of the symbolic objects that have been represented to the mind, as things that are opposed to their public representation as movable conditions that are condoned by the jurisdiction of municipal, provincial, regional, or state adjudications that are signified as a truth that appeals to the rights contained within the symbolic appearances as forms of truth in-themselves. In a world where the symbolization of existence is to become represented outside of its incarnation as a clarity of what reality has in common with those that are total to what might generate its possibility, what humanity does to protect reason from its dissolution into a dystopian plateau of uniformity, in collusion with administrative bodies that capture the symbols from their place of origin as appearances that should never be condemned to an obfuscation of the forms themselves as unifying moments of the symbolic into a totality of subjective emancipation, from horizons where the signifiers themselves represent the coordinates that propel reasonable social and political activity through the fray of its position into the disintegration of multiplicities in unified opposition and avoidance—subjectivity remains standardized to its objective unification with the symbolic as a moment that condoned the appearance as a formal adjudication to a reasonable stance to take where the conditions only appealed to state jurisdiction more than the public's common knowledge. The point of contention happens where the public has been seduced by a determinability that appropriates the truth by offering security and stability to all those for whom agreement is never too hard to achieve where concerns the sustainability of their own fiduciary interests being maintained by what appeals most to the public *en-masse*—people will simply save themselves before they risk the conditions of uncomfortable situations. But let us consider for one moment that this is never the case, that the actions of the most even-keel individuals are of an actuality biased toward ignorance, rather than the genesis of a position that had become of an inner reality that had represented more than what were possible of the limitations proposed by prudential wisdom alone; one for whom the projection of what would propel a constellation of objective unification with reality, forms a signifying moment generated by a symbolization that were proprietary to a particular subject where singular—yet universal to the totality of objectivity that had formed its possibility as a unifying moment of symbolization. The thrust of this condition repels its instantiation, through the torrent from where its original horizontal position of transcendence delivered a glimpse of truth to an individuality that would have otherwise been left within the obfuscation of the significations that had conjured what had been the quest of a spiritual undertaking, to always represent reality outside of the self-interests of commercial enterprise and administrable reality[55] as the soul of humanity; as never the place from where our essence is most vital and invisibly entwined with the concepts that compose a nature that brings more truth to the levels of consciousness than are knowable through a form of logic that is consistently being externally limited by global public institutions.

As for what is constitutive of the Cogito, we might presuppose that its state of self-awareness has a lofty position in consequential affairs of the former—as being is not quite itself where the Cartesian rapport that we sometimes possess between subject and world, is post-ontological in the manner that it is posited by the mind, but pre-ontological insofar as its conditional flux with reality is guided by speech (Lacan) as much as by the thoughts that circumvent *logos* itself. The in-itself of existence is within a structural compromise with the intentions that condition a Self—from its ontological positionality—toward a thrust of energeia that gathers the intentional subjects further, through the troughs of conscious self-awareness where the world is subjective only to an inward gaze that perceived its horizon as this which is actual to subjectivity. This may be something invisibly real within a glimpse offered the powers of an observing consciousness (Hegel), yet is part of the simplicity of ego formation that condoned a subjective formalization of the appearances guiding us through the riddles that are representative possibilities of the

[55] Based upon Adorno's concept in *Negative Dialectics* (Continuum, 1973) of the administered world. In essence, it refers to a position where society reflexively precedes a subject's own presuppositions about what is "out there", and that the world *vis-à-vis* society, is being monitored by invisible powers concerned with bio-political reality.

thing-in-itself—where the appearances have departed the scene for the other subject-object. If we might for a moment preconceive of the edificial, conceptual formalization of a noetic substrate, as Husserl had to the one posited by Marx as an inversion of the Hegelian dialectic, we may find ourselves amidst certain oceans of thought where we find a fluxion between the clarifying moment of ego formation as a reproducible subjective composition of the object; as a production-force of natural self-realization. What one must endeavor to accomplish in this quagmire of self-reflexive objectivities, is to conceptualize inner forms of thought, other than the self-reflexive subject-object interplay condoning that a thing-in-itself become more reflexive of a subject's own truth than the possibilities that originate in world-consciousness; as a measure of something that may then be reduced to its actuality as pure concept, leading toward a resolution of traumatic events and thoughts that have been gathered by a separation from the objective forms from whence they had originated. As subjects we are more prone to accept a delivery from the conditions of a safe state-of-affairs, into a network of social ties instrumental to the development of actual representations, than fantasies that originated in a repressive state of hyper-sexuality, for instance. Making matters worse, the same condition is offered to those that are found monitored by their own impotence to actualize a *jouissance* that would replenish the wells of pleasure, with something that would return the symbolic from its obfuscated inauthenticity. Toward a transcendent radiance that coordinated the genesis of what would drive from a soul the inner-most evils of bad faith, in order to reconstruct subjectivity to make allowances for the manner by which self-identity may be symbolized to Others, without becoming this for which no Self has an inner space of judgment, and unreasonable conditions to how the symbolic moment of ethical transcendence may support the necessary psychological repairs of consciousness—rather than instantiating a whole slew of representations that are hegemonic of their own emancipatory nature. The goal is to accommodate the claim that an emancipatory subjectivism, is natural to human progress, yet to propose limitations upon the psychological projections for which there may also be incarnations of those for whom the opening of the void to a world of phenomena, had broken subjectivity from an emancipatory condition of self-identity and progressive ego formation.

The *de facto* reality is that logos (language, speech), shapes a subject's internal relationship to the symbolic dimension—we must have words with those for whom silence is an observation of the truth, before we cancel all allowances made for those with whom disclosure through speech is more reifying. Yet, by these very means, one cannot avoid Wittgenstein's observation that speech must only be used when one knows what to say, acts as another twist of fate—for all coffee drinkers of the world had transcended the commonplace rituals of small efforts to gather more prospects for shopping rituals and identifiable fashion trends; lets one remain certain that nothing is to interfere with an necessary accommodation of rituals associated with hygienic practices (including the trimming of a beard).For must we not perceive ourselves from whence we had initially come, identifying the objectivity of a planet with primitive language so as to coordinate bodies with an environment in which they resisted or desired to dwell? Far be it from the ones for whom language is an art form that is reducible to constant silence, in agreement with a claim that appropriate conduct is more significant than making words count as much as the objects for which they stand—especially as years go on, utterances that have not seemed authentic expressions of necessary conditions of truth, formalize themselves within the real apprehensions shaping the subjective stance as an ultimate resource to where the symbolization of our experiences becomes of signifiers that we would wish to possess or erase, as time becomes the most significant component of what delivers us from the conditions that makes these signifiers that remain within our heads disappear—never to become representations of the things that once mattered to us most. While the objective compromise we performed with ourselves is accustomed to a place where thoughts reside, amidst a nouveau of symbolic representations, we must always remember what Lacan had suggested about the symbolic dimension—it is diachronic to the signified.[56] The

---

[56] Lacan, Jacques, *Écrits* (1966) *Éditions de Seuil,* (English trans. (2006, 2002) *W.W. Norton and Company, Inc.*) The essential idea that the symbolic dimension is clearly indicated as the ontological domain wherein phenomena co-exist as signifiers, promulgates the work of its author. That representations are posited as symbols within the temporalization of a subject in positional space, is particular to its diachronic instantiation as a posited *imago* upon the horizon. The insistence remains that the symbolic dimension only touches the real where it also engages the world as a totality to which subjectivity had become subordinated to its own ego transcendence.

lives that have crossed ours are only actively erased when we can no longer accommodate the representations that have developed from personal sacrifices or injuries to the conditions of this life, as the one that is to come should we reconcile the differential structures that might have been made edificial to the representations of what had propelled a subjective composition of collective self-identification, through its savage symbolization as an obfuscation of the realities that are never those transcending the symbolic space out to where productive and reproductive societal powers are engineering a development of nature in-itself.

As one may fully have within a capacity of the understanding to do so, the symbolic dimension is also part of a natural progress of symbolic meaning from its origins in Ancient and Medieval periods of our history. For us to consider for a moment the most profound depths of what history and architecture signify to us through these symbols—on days such as today when we see the latter engulfed in flames as in the case of the Notre Dame Cathedral—we can simply realize what is ablaze a consciousness that has for it a signification that is deeper than the considerations that psychoanalytic praxis may be fully capable of determining. For *logos*, an articulation of the conditions that monitor any such accidental events, that are to be etched upon the annals of history as incidents, for which there is no common explanation, so are the symbols that have been diachronically signified to a mind that is searching for a truth in a history more profound than the answers provided by administrable normativity. Within a world—sometimes exposed to a variability that gathers its measure in the souls of those that would anticipate another outcome than the one that had shaped the past—so are the moments of the present equally significant to the outcome of things that had become of an extraordinary set of circumstances, that were entirely beyond the scope of predictability. For instance, I might conceive of an object in the night that only stands in relation to my Self, yet where the idea of it becomes total to the productive activities of society, it becomes an act larger than the contemplation had initially *intended* itself to be. Johann Fichte articulates it best when he identifies causes as reflexive to each other in the book *The Science of Knowledge*.

One should always be most careful where concerns symbols with a religious connotation, as for these to be utilized to impose economic barriers throughout, is never well-received by the accidents of providence and all such unreasonable conclusions that might result from the same place of origin where the symbolic dimension had originated for humankind. For things that are natural such as Aristotle's elements—earth, air, fire, water (and the universal substance that accompanies them)—forbids a causal nature that is within the Cartesian duality, yet encumbers the matter-form relation in such a manner as to compel causality to be generated by naturalized components, standing in relation to the human elements that identify the signifying properties therein. We can of course also make reasonable attempts to see the chemical instincts in filiation with how enterprising *genus* is to represent *Being* as a composite of many elements that would exponentially increase a likelihood of causal *eventism*[57] being generated by the way the image appears to us and what were giving it powers of signification.

One can rightly imagine that the prospects dwelling deep within a collective body-politic, may also become causal to any such events, that had once been contained within movements that were identifiable as political or social causes, that had perceived a symbolization of what would give life to the projection of their radical autonomy—yet we might suggest that the wanderlust of the times, in which we have been more protected by our choices, and less protected by administrable bodies of the electorate, we emerged as a generation of those for whom the symbolization of what is the genus of the times—or more specifically our *genera*—is the internal relations that we might possess with the symbols of the past, as those for which progress toward the horizon is still somehow antiquated within a resurgence of the power of symbols that had accompanied the imaginings of those for whom the signifying composition of the world, is not reducible to one particular object through a controlled obsessional act. We become proponents of a symbolization that is biased toward potencies driven by dialectical conquests, that are propelled by the forces of nature, yet oftentimes would wish only to give meaning to the objects dwelling within our memory—that we would wish to totalize our own experiences for purposes that are proprietary to what delivers us from other evils of the universe—the ones that have taken on a newer form than had previously been known by religious scholars, or the like. A more secular world is now upon us, and the moment we look to

[57] A proprietary term that refers to exponential quantifiers that resonate through world phenomena—then become of the logical forms by which we come to address ourselves as subjects, coordinated by the exigencies of the spatial dimensions in which we are experienced as representable co-presences.

the symbols of the past as mere relics designed by Monarchies in possession of the means to rule a population, in order to stymy scientific discoveries, greater significance can be given to those artefacts that possess true historical meaning. An understanding that had formed a psychological transformation that has been initiated by the logic of our times though, still falls into the shadows of its own scientific potential; where it perceives the driving forces of nature to have been industrial control over sectors of the economy that should have been emancipated from industrial control, in order to return to the natural economic growth stimulated by post-industrial developments. The natural discourse that results from things that sustain the former as an independent body of economic activity in-itself—is related to the symbolic dimension insofar as there are individual consciousnesses in correspondence with such activity. For instance, the act of driving is never a performance that would require the images of a symbolic dimension in order to properly conduct the necessary set of decisions associated with the former, lest we rest assured that an accident is a variable that is there upon the horizons of possibility. The symbolic dimension is reserved for literature, philosophy and sociology, the arts, psychology, psychoanalysis, and architecture such as it offers these disciplines a mode of consciousness that is both based in the possibilities generated by the active imagination, just as it is the positings of one for whom the symbolization of something that is total to the world may incarnate a truth that is particular to a given historical event, to be perceived by those most receptive to an *eventism*[58] conjured by the totality of the circumstances that had made things come to pass.

Such as the world is a place where things always come to pass from the causal nature of a planetary evolution of ideas, the Cartesian cogito remains particular to emancipatory self-identities, searching for a meaning inside the wells of consciousness composing reality in-itself.

So it is this for which we are encompassing the will, toward a transcendence that supersedes the accomplishments of generations that have done nothing but give the necessary historical context, in which we might apprehend a dialectical progress, less ambulatory of precious political movements; yet altogether symbolically entwined with the concepts that formed their originary contact with the essences of humankind as a duality escaping binary complications—yet altogether

[58] Ibid., p.103.

still of a nature that composes an objectivity in filiation with its potencies within the eschatological context from whence they had originated. The presupposed condition that documents a concept of *humanity,* lest it be contemplative the an *eventism* symbolic to the genesis of what had propelled reality from the core of its symbolic instantiation—into a lexicon of sublimated attempts to subordinate subjectivity from a self-realization, projected from the existential nexus of activity coordinated from an internal regression of symbolic space—is by all means possible of a logic of an assemblage of ideas, in a point of contact with a periodicity that may only have originated from a logical form that had been generated by *history* in-itself. Such that there would be much ado where concerns structures that had originated upon horizons, where there is no confrontation with the doubts that have remained unaccompanied by the progress that supports their generative composition to the matters that condoned the more vital exponents of prudential discourse—and what is resourced from forms of conduct in filiation with higher ethical motives than would be particular to the their symbolic origins in the matter-form synthetic representations available to a progressive public sagacity—we are adumbrated by a content that is exposed in a disclosure to the symbolizations that accompanied dialectical abstractions of the forms; having become of existential compositions that determined the temporality of the thoughts that would only condemn capricious ontological activity to a dimension that Kant had reserved for a terrain that were considered illusory—to a conduct that would otherwise be of a totality that had become particular to the symbolic extensions of existentiality—becoming what appeared upon horizons beyond transcendence. Those that had been seduced by their formal observational consciousness within the very object of symbolic observation, by which it had been betrothed to an object of abstraction, most limited by the forms to which the presuppositions that accompanied them, would be transfixed within a rendering of existence outside of the natural composition of the matter-form synthesis to with which it had been encumbered. Thereto, the provisional abstractions that are more sagacious than the ones presupposed by pure economic activity, resonate within the symbolic dimension, as realities formed by a consciousness that had become toward its own observational authenticity, over the significations that are particular to the destinies that rivaled this for which no resolute human inequity is to survive the genesis that had progressed outside its temporal origins. Such as it is—and as it is ever to be—the composition of a collective, determines the possibilities of its subjects. Within this, in consideration of an experience that is symbolic to the former, we are subsumed within the conditions of the formalization of what had resonated within, as a profound possibility of abstract nature—confounded within the regions of a consciousness that had never possessed thoughts that had been more responsive to the origins from where the symbolic dimension had captured our minds, souls, and spirits transcending existence.

That this should be a space worth considering, as the dimension of the most profound regions of intellection, we would never reject for a certainty. However, how to compose subjectivity in symbolic awareness of where it is to become situated amidst a transcendence that had not discovered a truth within the dimension that had been granted us, is a sure pathway toward misunderstanding the totality from where it had originated. For it is in history that the symbols defining the context for which we would encounter ourselves as objects for which there stood a symbolic representation that identified us as beings, is never to be confused with the histories that made it possible to expose ourselves to such representations of a knowing mind. Lest we surprise the condition whereby we had been accompanied by a departure to the ground level of reality—where existential truth exposes our frailties, just as it does the strengths that even the most vulnerable may sometimes possess—it is only to realize that a juxtaposition of what composes symbolic identification as a means of recognition to the causes that project the experiences of subjectivity through the troughs of societal experience, into a reality that is shaped by the choices that have constellated within the consciousness of one individual, are quite particular to the auspices of a reflexive adjudication to which social practices gather the spiritual forms with which we are encumbered toward a consecration of the powers behind them—driving their responsible conduct throughout a dimension where good things are always within the realm of possibility. Yet so are the things that must remain undisclosed. The closing of the space, however, is a more serious operation that requires some labour-intensive contemplation—this for which courage becomes an asset driving all other assets away. It would be best to close the space with language—lest the remnants of our silence break the moulds wherein the truth of our souls go uncompromised by resistance to the thresholds that bind us to the core of an existential confrontation with our own sense of subjective apotheosis.

Such as it is, the manner in which we do depart a simulacrum of our own metonymic self-expression, the terms which define an inner sense that is determinable of a reality that is least conjured by the objective forms in which they had historically originated, are the same as the ones from which our empirical identities are never more likely to capture under the conditions where *logos* had become a subordination of a composition of the actualities that condoned the abstractions made possible by a verisimilitude to the concepts, that may only be defined by the dialectically productive capacities of an authenticated existential being-in-itself.

The viability of the actions that project any such identical Self throughout the outer regions of ontological experience, are motivated by a conception of the very things that are to insure that the actualities are to become abstractions at the nexus of logical possibility—answers to what had compelled the internal dimensions of consciousness to become entwined with the questions that have met with a responsive verifiability. We would only succumb to an obfuscation of the reproductive powers that dwelled within, where compromises had tethered upon the choices of legislative powers that had administrable authority over the juridical insights, provided through an authentication of the content posited by a process that had determined the same outcome as the collective identities that had been instantiated through symbolic gestures reduced to particular forms of conduct.

As chance would have it, these forms of conduct also determine the natural progress that is to ensue, in a manner by which causes that had once been ineffectual to their moment of symbolization as a purposive reality, are instantiated by a logic that had driven away the transcendence of where the ego is particular to authenticated subjects as actualities responsive to their objective counterparts—and abstractions of the symbolic dimension to others participating upon the terrain where a transcendence of self-identity had founded its position, and a commensurability with its object—constitutive of this for which cogent endeavors sanctioned by humankind become conquests to the imagination, as well as salient experiences of their eventuality within the logic of the real.

That we would adopt for one moment the simple conclusive appeal to the appearances that had originated from their horizontal origins—if things were as the necessities of dialectical abstraction would have them be—we would certainly be fully capable of presupposing an identifiable form to which one would be able to ascribe a dimension for symbolization that had become particular to the actualities of subjective experience; from a mediated point of historically objective perspicuity—projecting a conceptual content that had been composed by its transformation of an identical Self into a symbolic reality.

Within the moment we have recognized our symbolization in and *through* the Other, the matter-at-hand becomes of this which transcends the symbolic space into which we are entwined, or in synthetical unity, as Kant would have had it; though the dimension had conclusively been structured to be illusory in dialectical transcendence of the abstractions possible *a priori* of the objects-in-appearance. Certainly, we must superimpose upon the eternal will of Kant, a conceptual datum with which he had fashioned the dynamical observances within the context of which our appeals to the real, are only conditioned by the regulative nature of what had been posited through the instruments of transcendental observation in-themselves. Nonetheless, never should it become of superstition that we accommodate the appearances as they resonate the inner space of what illuminates us in beauty, or in confrontation with the things that stand opposed to what compels the psychical forms composing the self-identity to which we have committed ourselves.

For some, the Schopenhauer principle of sufficient reason had become a verifiable resource to a causality that would initiate life choices, in coordination with the objects that had been symbolically entwined with the intentional purposes of the Other; and thereto the abstract possibility that we had made a mistake is entirely ruled-out, as the symbolic observances made throughout the significations made by an irrefutable co-presence of absolute judgements, is representative of the change that must become of our involvement with the Other, as a being to which we may distribute a sense of fellowship and an equal formation of what posits the self-identical forms of being; to which we condone our subjective activities throughout the symbols to which we have become attached, as such.

As objects-in-themselves, said representations of the mind are known to be provoked mostly into despair, should they be sullied by the Other through acts that have deigned to resign self-identity to an inferiority that resonates within a complex formed through a resolute sense of inadequacy—resounding upon the world stage as this from which the Self had not yet transcended the limitations proposed by an over-arching body-politic that had identified within a class of inferior intellects—however, where we assert a dialectical imposition to fulfil a thrown spirit from its grounding within the essence of an *ousia* resolute within its subordination of the dimension from which it had originated—we coordinated an appeal to the heavens, from which these appearances were once known to have become symbolizations of the eschatological figures resonating through a collective theocracy of figures that would generate representations that we would now consider entirely removed from their originary historical placement as the signifiers to which our judgments are formed, through the faculties that we have been granted by some divine right-of-passage.

The appearances in-themselves, are precisely these by which all other existences resonate as things-in-the-world, for we derive a subjective appeal to the manner by which observances of the symbolic dimension are conclusive of another side to the appeal: This which emits a radiant transcendence particular to subjectivity, while being entirely in communion with the images representing a totality that resounds within the experiences of one mind, that had become in-itself more than it may have been, should the Self have presupposed that the significations resonating within being, were not identical to humankind's reflections that had originated in reality. The perceptions generated by the understanding are resolute to the dimensional context in which they had originated, or particular to the concepts formalized through what had initialized self-identity; as the mode of verifiability wherein the context instantiated the symbolic identification with which a Self is projected as a totality of the Otherness within which the Self had been symbolically obfuscated. A departure for a being-in-itself is propositional to the presupposition that its own self-identity, will only be preserved through the logic of Otherness, should it have posited being as the Other to which the Self acts in correspondence, through a unified performative activity that had not subordinated the symbolic dimension into an obfuscated condition; standing opposed to the proprietary aims of ethical experience as the immediate coordinates of self-identity.

One would be no more willing to have private self-interests moving through our minds, than participating in an excursion that documented the becoming of acts of global war, controlled by a dentist that were intent upon the restructuring of our very own teeth by whichever means possible. So we can rightly say, that the symbolic dimension is particular to subjectivity and self-identity, and that the Other to which it corresponds is never to become particular to the content of the being-in-itself, by the very proclamation that emancipatory justice is better situated without the appropriation of those for whom the door had been opened by economic privilege, and personal or professional self-interest. But back to the more significant matters that are to become particular to the quest for a radical abstraction of the beauty that is posited by its total representability, from a horizon where ethical transcendence resonates in possibility, and captures the origins of where meaning is to be realized through the signifiers of image-objects that foretell of humankind's beginnings as psychological species-beings, with full ego formation happening alongside the placement of what had posited the spaces where the more destined roots of our natural transformation into creatures with a concrete universality exist well within reach.

Let us presuppose that the thieves of this world, are all ready and waiting to pounce upon the objects of our own contemplation—with full intent to collect their own sense of proprietary justice, to the spaces in which these representations of the mind dwell. Would we not there despair that these Others that have sacrificed ethical transcendence to self-interest, and greed had become particular to the same illumination that had been such a significant component of the inner Self that we would hasten to imagine something horrible to become of them? Certainly, we must care for our Others as we do ourselves under given conditions—one would not just simply shoot a barking dog because it had interrupted a peaceful afternoon of contemplative activities. So we are conditioned toward a stand-still—a deadlock of no-nonsense variability. Though we toil within instinctual reason to exude rationality at every available opportunity, another human instinct is to annihilate the source of our troubles to the very core of its own existence. Truthfully, this instinct were particular to those that held favour with the Darwinian challenges of natural selection, before we had developed a sense of humanity that had reached beyond the brute forces of nature, developed by an industrial context where they shaped the personalities that philosophy would wish to eliminate from the mind, wherever the chance presented itself to us.

Given our new found freedom and possibility to pursue an emancipatory horizon of beauty, intellection, aesthetics, ontological discovery, and ethical societal representation, we would be glad to end relations within any such persons that were to jeopardize these positions—only from the point-of-view that the coordinates of poor taste, must never become sacrifices for the self-identities that are projecting something of greater philosophic integrity or ontological purposiveness. We must reject all those for whom the affords of our natural self-realization is modulated by the superficiality of an irritating and classless societal group overwrought with the sensibility of a pursuit of capital—without respect to the symbols throughout history that have led us down the path where the truth did not belong to a public thief, that were hell-bent upon removal of the developments that were attainable beyond the scope of the totality of their lives, and well into the next century, if natural planetary development were not obfuscated by these wretched criminals that would never lead us back toward the light that had birthed a prosperity that had to be earned by the correct means alone. Not the articulations of those possessing abhorrent distortions in a contorted savage intellect. What needs be undone, is those for whom the ethical natures of higher moral individuals than the ones pursuing private economic advantage, must fall out of the scope of the way that the history of humankind may be depicted upon the world stage. The failing of this enemy, is now top priority to all those willing to divide the truth from its signification as something that emits pure evil and must never see the light of day, and to achieve a radical enlightenment possible of justice, where the aims of the public had once wished that discourse had defined societal development never biased to industrial development; and an abstraction of the wells of aesthetic radiance that must appear only to those within the framework of psychological transcendence—formed through the contents of the real spiritual beings that determined a greater good for the ones that found a common purpose in these very ideals.

However, it is better to *signify,* is it not? By way of dialectical reasonability alone, I find it comprehensible to posit the existence of a most fortuitous panoply of representations generated through the mind to be a more exhilarating experience, than things within the gaze having no linguistic signification of vitality or interest. Where we begin, is where it all seems to end, in the safety of a reality that binds us to how the possibility of an engagement with the public where concerns the former is not always to be desired. How then, are we to be total and complete as beings responsive to the objects situated within our interior space? I will maintain that the positing of objects as coordinates to which the signifiers are in correspondence—not as Other than a Self, but particular to the Self through its symbolic identification—I believe, would wish for Lacan's support in the matter, since we oftentimes would wish that there be no Other; though on this point he vacillates between observances of the possibility/impossibility of a psychical Other, other than the Self. As for Johann Fichte, we know the not-self to be quite constitutive of the Self or the "I", yet we are always surprised as it posits things that had not yet occurred to us, as though they had been particular to our own self-identity—without us even making the realization. Granted, the position from where we generate subjective aims at its annihilation, a not-self may be consequently reflexive to our own well-being. So it is from this that one would insist that a self-analysis be undertaken so as to generate a state-of-affairs that re-posits the cogito, as though the signifiers were related only to the objects in architectonic space—within the coordinates of a symbolic domain—as contingent articulations to the similar fashion where the simulacrum would appear to those that perceived abstract space as symbolic, rather than appearing as noumenal presuppositions in projection of subjective wills.

However, as appearances are by nature dialectical, I would also endeavor to perceive objects within the symbolic dimension, based upon a dialectical abstraction of the thing-itself. Such that it would become of possibility, it is certain that things must be total to the concepts formed by the content of the mind, and representative of the intentional object to which my contemplation would be able to presuppose an object, simply through the act of positing it, as Husserl had. What I have done, is to add a dialectical projection to the conceptually signified as its nominal composition, thereby establishing a noematic context in which the syntactical observances of the objects where they exist, may be perceived within a given temporal and ontological framework. Should this be in correspondence with productive activities taking place within the given framework—as a totalization of the possibilities governing the enterprises of what resides there upon horizons of thought—I apprehend that no one will be to set adrift their reproductive activities being developed within a natural quotidian framing of the real world as a total experience—throughout a symbolic dimension that is intersubjectively entwined between the Self and conceptually signified modes that compose an understanding.

Though through appeals to the metonymic significations readily diagnosable of said powers of comprehension, we may certainly become of our objects, just as they may become of us—the ontological objects with which our psychological state is inherently *metonymic* in principle. As we have the metonymy, metaphor, and synecdoche of the ever-too-comprehensible French post-Structuralists—a resistance to which is now part of a transformation in North-America, in particular Canada. We do depart of wisdom where it is to suggest that the natures that determined our subjective experience, become expunged by inconsequential political artifices that ultimately only undermined the signifiers responsive for their own instantiation as possibilities of dialectical intellection. Such that *Being* is both rationally and radically opposed to a natural exposition to the matters determinable of the categories transcending rational judgment, from their prospective original point-of-contact within the significations of an undulating self-identity, that were resonating within the significations themselves—as oblique and despondent representations that had become of immediacies prone to the abstractions that had conferred with modulated aesthetic originations in thought—a correspondence that is derived within the recognition of metonymic ideation, is determinable of its abstract origins from the totality that had instantiated non-identity. So becoming particular to the composition of what subjects dialectically presupposed, before the general context in which the superposition that had universalized self-identity had been recognized both within the universal and the symbolic dimension. Where the former would be singular to a noetic stratum of vertical consciousness—and the latter of a noematic constitution that had identified self-identity as original to its symbolic instantiation as a totalized unification of its representative propriety, posited upon the primordial terrain—all such horizontal observances become a dialectical context in which the particular compositions of symbolic identity discovers the truth of its own existential reality.

The latter forms a consequential mode of being, determinable to a state in which proprietary aims apportioned to self-identity are limited by the representability of the subject's own objective reflexivity. In other words, subjectivity builds a rapport with its existential truth as particular to its own cogito, yet universal to its existentialization[59]—for the moment the positional context in which a subject has been symbolically entwined with its existential responsibility, the coordinates of the socio-political context determinable to the form of the content that is representable and perceived by another subject, is within a context where a public or collective responsibility becomes part of the *spirit of the people.* So designed are the interstices where intelligible differences are known as consequential to plateaus of the authoritative judgments that govern responsibility; as a concept shaped through powers imposed upon individuality, by the objective conditions reasoned as legislative controls of the subjects' identical Selves—conclusively leading to stratifications of individuality—led by a false sense of agency over the symbolic space, where an individual possesses access to their very powers of emancipatory value; and a structural transcendency of limitations imposed by the body-politic, already in possession of internal conflicts within the community itself. The rituals that govern participation in which individuals find a larger social context for projections of the Self—never to become violations to the symbolic space in which others may dwell—is prior to the content where such spaces are coordinated movements, to accept a radical scission between the substance of the people, and the support for individual freedoms that necessitate a more horizontal order to the symbolic terrain, in which the inner Self achieves its very emancipatory justice in-itself.

For all intents-and-purposes, Husserl's *pregiven* world[60] is universal to a particularity that is never confronted by oppositions from its particular wills, where what had been revealed, through a flawed universalized structure imposed upon self-identity, is a natural component of total being. Yet to suggest that distributive justice is the continual appropriation of self-identity, and emancipatory justice had long been a feature common to administrable reality—is the state where economic balance is determined by the factions in possession of power, and to make an appropriate argument for a projection of a revolutionary dialectical potency, pivotal to the changes that one must create within the world, little by little. One will notice how ontological liberty can readily be

---

[59] As though the universal may be *universalized*, this which if existential might also be *existentialized*.

[60] Husserl, Edmund. *The Crisis of European Sciences and Transcendental Phenomenology* (1970).Northwestern University Press.

associated with psychosis in a certain dimension that makes psychoanalysis still necessary; but we can also appreciate the *de facto* reality that sometimes the actions of one whom has avenged self-identity, in order to reconcile being with its own symbolic identity, has been caused by an individual's ownership over a potential that defines human subjectivity—capable of attaining prosperity more readily when it had not been excluded from the justice that had determined the freedoms belonging to administrable conditions that have been instantiated as limitations upon the naturalization of human substance, into its condition of wholeness and self-realization. From the moment of symbolic representation, to the totalization of spiritual authenticity, with which an emancipated subject has broken-out from an oppressive qualitative state-of-being, self-identity becomes a transcending power within a natural, progressive state of awareness that situates subjectivity within its original position of resistance to a body-politic, that has dominion over subjectivity as an individuated Being. With this it would seem subjectivity is contained within itself as a being that has been deprived of its natural rights, and therewith the symbolic dimension does not have access to the provisional givens of collective identity—such would be the case where the state had behaved unethically. The will of the people, such as would be the regions where reside subjective compositions, provisional to those for whom purchasing power is a collective community assertion, gather their structural compromises for affluent members of society, all sharing in the attributes of a self-identity that has been restructured to the advantage of others, and toward their own condition of loss. With this in mind, it is not enough to reform a natural Self, in order to comply with the administrable conditions posited by objectivity; but to establish a context in which emancipatory justice may return a subject to its condition of social and political awareness—without being confronted by the economic imbalances that deign to presuppose the failure of a subject from the attainment of its own objectives.

A symbolic terrain—where any such matters identifiable of a justice that is administrable by a logic that had not confronted a Self through its own identical resource of *Being*, thrusts upon subjectivity an imperative that casts-out the social context where agency, transcends its formal limitations as an object determinable of the causal objectives determining a being-in-itself.

What is representable to being, by its state of authentic juridical symbolization, is ownership over a position that it had inherited from a natural progression through symbolic spaces, coordinated from a transcendence into subjectivity—beyond the administrable forms that had divided being from a completion of the Self that had been pregiven self-identity as a dimension of the symbolic context in which subjects would have first been administered a natural composition of reality, administrable to the gaze of another symbolic Self. Such as it is, the latter is the signified, and the object of thought to the perceiving Self that encounters this oftentimes through cognitive gifts diagnosable as powers of perception that add a natural and instinctual quality to *Being*.

So it is that the savants of the world have been put in possession of this for which many treasures may be discovered, yet also images composed of nightmares that no one would wish upon even their worst enemies. The fragility if humankind *depends* upon the givenness of the manner in which the symbolic dimension is depicted as a function of truth, and never through a bungler with a failing artificial soul, seeking a form of satisfaction that will only mislead a population, from the aestheticization of what would render public awareness to a strength that would even defeat the frailties of the obfuscating darkness, that is sometimes prone to befall an ailing planet as we search for greater meaning. A wider, more responsive sense to the objects that define us as beings, that have been activated by cultural instantiations of the natural progress that condones a content that is in possession of a more broad scope of social vision than the development of the signs, distributed through the landscape whereupon we are determinable by our own projected natures—or an apoplexy that undermines the common spaces, is never to be discredited before we concede certain aspirations to the authentication of what propels humanity forward is thrust upon us by thinkers such as Nietzsche. [61]

As philosophers, we may concede to the latter a realm of impossibility that is natural to the progress that is definitional to the context in which said ideals are to be discarded as lofty claims, yet what "truth" has in its possession, is an identifiability of mysterious synchronicities that are

---

[61] Such as it is and ever it would become—that he were inextricably intertwined into the beauty and the search for individuation from the industrial consequences of Schopenhauer's work, we must persevere in pursuit of the same individuation of Self, as had been recognized by the late *Freud*.

often readily disavowed as mere coincidences. Lest there be any confusion that remains, the espousal of the egregious errors that undermine our symbolic operations, with the syntactical forms from which we developed a reality that is particular to an embodied spiritual collective, there is nothing to renounce other than these where faults are particular to the negotiations, that any of the latter's members confer with reality in such a manner, as to become deceived by a structural opposition to the formalization of which significations are most verifiably in filiation with the objects (signifieds) that accompanied them.

The spiritual ground, where an occupancy of the primordial terrain of this planet—through the discretion of nation-states and provincial boundaries localizing the phenomena in sociation with world phenomena—becomes more determinable of cause, where the naturalization of the process by which reality transcends an intersubjective quantifier to the dialectical impetus to reproduce a subjective truth from its intersubjective auspices as a form of knowing, evocative of both the spirits that had elevated capricious natures from their whims, while condoning the progression of knowledge through a space where material objects are entwined with the phenomena that give these things their ontological signification—as Schopenhauer were clear to point out: "The will is the in-itself of its own phenomenon."

It would seem, had it never been particular to human nature that a representation be within the cranium itself, so we find Hegel's dialectical progress toward a mediated universality to propose nothing aporetic—identical to a subject from its natural objective composition. However, philosophy must be hermeneutically assessed as a combination of a teleological component that determines it to be a necessary practice, as such. The symbolic dimension belongs to neither inextricably; and so I resist taking sides, at risk of a discovery that the contradictions inherent of a "negative dialectic" would haunt the very dimension to which unmediated practices become particular to a Self in search for Nietzsche's observation that one must "Know Thyself!".

The delight that is offered to philosophy, is the sense of where a variability in commitments to one concept of scholarship or the other, enters into the very cancellation of the possibility of a synthesis taking place—that with the proper care might actually bring vision to the phenomena that have been interpreted for twenty-five centuries, while leading down many paths to an unfinished human endeavor. Perhaps, a synthesis of ideas, is precisely what the world either desperately needs, or will altogether rule outside-of-reality; as from where things stand, the will to resist the *status quo*, or to repeat the doctrines of the great masters, seems at times to leave things to the past, rather than to deliver them a future yet still beyond our grasp.

Given that the walls existing between us are more prone to become opened to something beyond what will come to represent an authenticity to the modes of reality that we might wish to address as primordial beings, while remaining particular to the autonomy of the symbolic dimension, such syntheses proposed a critical mass that is daunting to those in pursuit of which truth may be *posited* by the mind, as a presupposition of the thing-in-itself, and one that is involuntarily given by an unintelligible monster of cognitive thought—the residuum of a gravitas that had possessed only the bravado to project an historical perpetuation of the unconditional finitude that had remained within systems of thought that had relegated subjectivity to a delusive form of awareness. Such is the illusory nature of a public consciousness that had become ensconced within its own rationality and particularities—given that the attempt to exclude all binary oppositions from the cogito, to its formation as a property of its own symbolization—the condemnation of aporetic relations with syntheses that had been formed, without a careful projection of the variability with which they stand in opposition, is to compose a subjectivity saddled with a confusion that needs be willed away, by its own representability and reflexive self-identification. An epistemological break with the phenomena that resist the coordinates from where the syntheses between philosophical positions exist, is not the voice or representation that is identical to a subject. One must omit the things that are fused, in order to seclude the Self in the nests of an in-itself, that is reflexively entwined within ownership of the properties determinable by a natural substance determining qualitative being.

Such that *being-qua-being*, has resisted the urge to unify with the oppositions that had instantiated a negative condition through its own signification, the impossibility that coordinates the projection of a Self, in filiation with an external source of the existential boundaries composing reality, where subjectivity confers its self-concept with the presence of the Other, the latter dissolves into a mist—as the Self had constructed Being as a posited *suchness*—bound by its own idiosyncrasies into a natural progression from matter to form; from content to existential truth.

With this we are never to concern ourselves with the rituals at stake, in opposition to the reflexive substance that is extrinsic to the horizon of the very consolidation of our own cognitive designs.

While never at a loss to posit which ontological form they must take, we must ascertain that what composes subjectivity, is this from which a mode of perception is neither an identity of a Self, nor is it a self-identity that is identical to its own perceiving Self as other than the Self. In order to remain within the confines of this project, we must self-realize the concept of what we are in fact, as identical to ourselves—yet find completion within the notion that our represented Self is merely a version of this that radiates the Self throughout what gazes upon subjectivity as the essence of Being, and the nature of a soul borne from corporeal matter, projected upon the landscape of our inner well-spring of ontological symbolization—gathering a place upon the horizon that we may call our own, once we have called to arms a position that collects the boundaries of what is truthful of existence, and posits it where it is one with nature. The pact that we have sealed with a wholeness that is only fragmentary, is relinquished to the symbolic identity for a plurality of a multi-dimensional reality, where subjectivity is in agreement with governances bound to a truth, that becomes representable to the reproduction of an awareness resonating an illumination of what radiates symbolic recognition.

The object that is formed from an instantiation of the Self, is open to a projection of identity that is constitutive to the symbolic identification that is posited by a perceiving mind, through an abstraction of its conditions within the other consciousness as this which perceives, and this which is to appear. Such that the Self is an appearance in a shadowed wilderness of its own otherness, a backdoor unveils something that posits an entry into a chamber that discloses being to a perceiving subject. In the Heideggerian sense, a revelation betrothed to Hegel has exposed the Self to its transformative capacities, naturally realized by a symbolization of this from which the inward glimpse posited matter through form as an intelligible means of intersubjective relations. Symbolic spaces—where images consolidate being into a natural composition of matter and form, resolute toward signifiers that have disappeared in order to position inward reflections of the mind behind walls of existence—are knowable to reality, and post-ontological to a composition of fading significations into a symbolization of its inner spiritual transcendence.

Such that the content of the latter is a construct of the mind and its totality, in response to the condition established through a projection of Self, as identifiable entities composed only of objective form, we might presuppose that the intelligibility of this position must be considered more succinctly—as a totality conducive to proper ego formation must be posited as a distantiated construct to social productivity—and never instantiated as a normative structure to ego identity, that will invariably counter its position as something constitutive of a Self. As exponents of the dialectical process may more subtly be composed of those for whom identity is the content of a subject's own symbolic space—and a structure of the mind that persists, while faced beyond the conclusive appeal to a totalizing force motivated by the global crises that may appear upon the doorstep of every citizen paying attention to the world such as it is—a resistance to the performances of post-industrial capitalism is procreative and reifying to the totality that they represent; while the technology that supports them are the institutions that deliver a message that is heard in silence by one poor soul, that must bear the burden of the world's problems without ever receiving worldwide acclaim. By mediating the responses of ego formation to an appropriation of ego, psychoanalysis fails to administer self-identity as its own power of mediation through its signifiers, becoming responsible for the absence of a field of view that establishes the necessary context in which the mind-soul may transcend said totality, motivated by an extravagance of a consumption of humanity, as an invisible commodity to be exploited for their subjective content as beings-in-themselves. A necessary return to a symbolic terrain, always situates the absence of joy with a visible transposition of an identical context in which the Self may project toward horizons—transforming the totality of a subject into a reproducible Self—bringing reality into a realm of spiritual awakening, that does not presuppose the content of a subject to consist of mass-appeal; and a quantity of being that is beyond this for which a naturalized symbolic identity, would ever become what ontology must be in order to sustain philosophy toward our future. From a condition readily diagnosable as a presupposition from which no adequate positing of the world would deliver a necessary compromise to reality, that had been subjugated through an apprehension of the conditions observed of the *de facto* truth in which the coordinates of a Self had transcended symbolic limitations—we must project something more radically entwined with extensions of Being that narrate an intersubjectivity monitored only throughout its own possible signifiers. Within a proposition that material forms outlay an essentialist conception to the former, self-identity reconciles with a moment where the naturalization of human becoming gravitates toward a circumstance that navigates itself toward a position where it is ever to dwell—a space where this by which we are conceived arrives; within the potencies from which our conceptions discovered the propositions that diluted our givens, into symbolic co-presences with the social forms representing the natures from which they had been constituted.

While establishing a pretext from which Being is provisional to the latter, the appearances framed within mind, become constitutive of a subjective sense of joy—uncompromised by the factors that undermine their reality as images, resolving to a context wherein they might evoke a delusive formalization of the source of reality from where they had been derived. I must insist—provided that a social imagination would never replace the reality possible of an actuality to symbolic ontological experiences—we surmise that the fictions that are in existence, are transgressions of an absence determinable by a misled sense of doubt; underneath the guidance of a despotic intellect driven by self-sustaining precepts that grant wishes only to those administered powers, driven by the profit motive. The *powers of perception* are never administrable gifts, donated to public enterprises that coordinate the scrutiny of those for whom the "good fight" is reason to keep pushing forward, through the troughs of a substance that would otherwise have dissolved into inequity and an absence of sustainability—such that the latter would be this from which no constitutive admissions of guilt would recognize a Self beyond its boundaries—fully responsible and necessarily awakened to the conditions that determined the projections that had inhabited an earnest and founded natural sense of reality so as to further action and its cause.

Insofar as a dialectical resource formalizes the internalization of the rapport we possessed with its counterpart in subjectivity, identity symbolizes itself beyond. A resource determinable of the Self, transcends the coordinates from where it had emerged—resonating through an object of the mind that signifies the origins from where it had been borne unto reality. We are determinable of the very same things that may have imposed determinations upon ourselves—reflexive objectives of the mind-world are subordinations of a universalized social psyche—

sometimes in possession of a free will that is detachable from the results of its own symbolic actualities. With this, we are actual to the singularity by which choices project toward the very universal form in which they may become constitutive of events beyond the actualities of Self. From the primordial terrain—to the symbolic condition that determines an actuality that is within the causal *nexus* of an abstract possibility—existence resounds where it furthers the lexicon of juridical propositions, acting within the coordinates of what instantiates a *logos* identifiable to *Being*.

Such that the object of being, is an instantiation of what posits the Self—without an apotheosis of subjective object formation becoming a necessity—it becomes apparent that the symbolic domain had left the subjective modality in which it had formed the object as a thing acting in liaison with the symbolic identity, that were to become a projection of itself upon the perceiving otherness; to which object formation had established an *a priori* connection. So as to reconcile the two, such that the other would be within the purview of subjectivity, it is that the content posited through the manifold to which a symbolic appearances may become real, is particular to the projection from where self-identity had emerged as a concept to the understanding. With this, the soul-substance becomes something transformative of the syntactical forms by which it had discovered the process of identification, as a content never to be lured by the presuppositions of an object-in-representation of a signified void of content. Alongside this, a precondition where subjectivity becomes more responsive to a content's natural progression of what becomes transpositional[62] to ego formalization as the symbolic enterprise, from which we entered into exchange as particularities—coordinated by mutual responses to the causes that determined the interplay from whence this correspondence had become realized—the Self reconstitutes itself, as a complete personality that is only to be conditioned by its situation as a thing that had transcended the boundaries from where subjectivity might have been within a political deadlock—where an abstraction of Self is transferred from its original instantiation as a being of fulfilment—to a soul of recognizable authenticity, that it had transcended this that had become disingenuous to the conditions of the material forms, which had

[62] The concept that transcendence is non-positional—yet posited upon the horizon as a transcendent positionality that has become intersubjective with a positional Other to which self-identity has become particular.

dialectically presupposed a calibration of subjectivity, established through what had perpetuated the appearances to which it might have become symbolically attuned.

From the immanence of ego formation, we are more constituted through an attribution to Cartesian thought, than its Hegelian condition as an extension to the Other—while the absolute subject posited by Hegel intersects with a condition whereby subjectivity pays tribute, to a deification of an objectively constituted self, in possession of propositions gathering conditions of subjectivity that become objectively ratified throughout; and subjectively ratified through Descartes. Alas, one should observe the *ego* as a phenomenon that could establish to whom it does truly belong. Where we might readily constitute ourselves as objects, search no further than the authentically savage wills of those for whom *ego* formation would never be sacrificed to its position upon the tables of regret and infinite longing for a past, that had compelled Marx to make his irrefutably radical positions known throughout the world. But is it in *this* world, where which we reside as passengers of a series of conditions becoming immanent—as reflections of a social psyche that dominates the evocation of this that might drive the corporeal conditions prone to humankind to a crossroads—where its repairs were to become features of the collective social psyches, in which objective forms had transformed a Hobbesian state of nature away from the labyrinth of despotism and radical upheaval, through the very presuppositions of a humankind that had proposed to rigidify a condition to humanity what is steeped in antiquated traditions biased toward abstract determinations? Or are the concepts that had formed those in possession of a reality that propelled a degeneration of society forward, more than its existential truth had composed of the provisional establishment, in an intelligentsia that had been renounced by populism to be those never in possession of a "free will" to humankind. However, in order that we condition an availability to the latter, it is that we resign popular culture to the pages of magazines, pulling the trigger on rationalism, without considering the consequential state that might become a reality to humanity; and continuing to project an authentication of a retinue more radical than thoughts would ever have become—disturbed through the capricious and overstimulated minds that had transferred a superficiality that made nothing of progress where concerns the meta-ontology with which we had become estranged. As those for whom immanence of Being, transcendence to the conditions from a determinability that had been modulated through a mediation of its place within a foe—rather than this from which we had attained a radical synthetic transformation—we perceive those from which a thing-in-itself (as Fichte would have made us believe is the letter of the law), as a reality that projects what is causal to subjectivity upon its object only insofar as the latter may do the same to us in turn. Were we to thrust ourselves upon a recourse that had inhabited the necessity of positing our imagined selves toward something more than what may be within the conditions of one from whom authenticity is never conceivable of the path toward justice as self-determination, hesitating to leave behind the very convictions that had given humanity its identifiable characteristics since the dawning of thought as an identity constitutive to the Self, into its apprehension as a symbolic entity—identifiable to the Other as constituted by its positing of a total being only identifiable within universality through its particularized symbolic signification?

Ergo, as a species-being, we become what we transcend, and must also transcend what we are to become, in order to attach ourselves to the coordinates of the horizon situating social stratifications of abstract possibilities, where the designs of public signification are instantiated as a concrete existential totality posited beyond the walls; and into the perception of those for whom the productive world is universal to the whole of the necessary pursuit of humanity's ontological transformation. In order to escape what betrays all conscious activity with an actuality that is outside of the systems of thought necessary to human production, we project a realm of symbolic actuality that is within the means of those for whom justice ends, where an appropriation of being to which subjects discovered a coherence to their own self-identities, is a concept forbidden to the furtherance of the doubt that accomplished nothing other than to subordinate the lifeworld to a position where planetary constellations of the noetic strata resonate, through beatitudes of a sublimity that proliferate the symbolic space, with a content more riveting than anything transcending its horizon—from where symbolic phenomena evaporate into the ether and are propelled into the void of an abyss.

Just as the light upon the ceiling, or the shadows of an obfuscating glimpse into the alleyways, where darkness feels as though an illuminating moment would be a transcendence of the spirit with which humanity were bound to become signified as a conceptual Self—

awakened and fully constituted in its subjectivity as a being-in-and-for-itself—we a more apt at this from which a self-positing had been endured only for so long as philosophy would be able to hold a thing-in-itself as constitutive to the otherness from whence it had originated; and given a distantiated totality of horizontal possibilities, from where subjectivity is to emerge as a symbolically constituted being-for-self, that were willing of an agency unhindered by the fixations of populism; generated by an overstimulation of a consumeristic and consumptive capital marketplace. Just as in Horkheimer and Adorno's masterpiece, *Dialectic of Enlightenment,* the subterfuge from a culture that wills only to consume social progress and political transformation in-itself, is of the particularity of a massive meta-critical evaluation, and valuation of the representations amounting to an absence of progressive economic activities—never determined by any other art form than this from which the radical cubists such as *Picasso*, for instance, had birthed an early 20th Century post-modern eclipse of the rationalism that had dominated the age in which the leitmotif of the time, may have been disturbingly light-hearted of the actualities to the former. Social reproducibility is perpetuated more by its ontologically symbolic content, where it is compelled by the actualities that have been projected from the medial forms, positing their potencies as the significations that have become real to the objects capable of forming the content reproducible of its socio-ontological instantiation.

Such that we might position ourselves, where the guardianship and responsibility of existential realism is particular to the latter, it is well within our capacities socially, to transcend the boundaries where the effects of symbolic experience propose dialectical limitations upon the Self; and a necessary projection that actuates causal structures within the logical framework where we reside as ontological co-presences—situated within the resolve of our consequential acts, and political efforts to subordinate subjectivity as a thing-in-itself that were without a truth that may have posited being, with a greater intensity than were possible of a concomitant relation to a Self that had not yet transformed being with the same degree of authenticity than the particular symbolic spaces were to require, in order to accommodate a projection of Self—such as the gaze becomes reflexive to self-identity; and subordinated horizons from where a Self might have become a noematic representation to a perceiving Other. Such that this is best supplied by those that are well-represented within a reproducibility that is endemic of a theoretical analyses where concerns cinematic representability, we must become those from whom the necessary observances of aesthetic transformation, become an equal component to the ontological framework of where the structural forms accompanied by the latter, are conceived as symbolically real enterprises within a restructured, controlled environment becoming an "arena" where such formalizations of imagined, objectified subjects, and transformed throughout the virtual field of consciousness in well-constructed, conceptual sequences that order rationalism within a modality that is particular to the symbolic context from where it had originated.

For ontology, as a structural formalization that conditions the possibilities of existential symbolization, are these from which the resonating properties may transition from their position situated in content, in order to reproduce a projection from where the more tragic forms of dialectical behavior conceded their form to the content that had conceived of the primordial conditions where self-identity is cast-out from the in-itself—toward the horizon as a *tragical* form. One must become of this from which the subordination of the enlightened natures that are posited, through careful observances of the projected terrain from where they had been generated, are conceptual totalities only to the horizontal existences that are posited—transcending the symbolic spaces where they had become co-presences—as noumenal representations concomitant to an image-object projected by a noematic referential calibration, constitutive of socio-ontological awareness. Such that this is existential to *Being*—as an existent of the compositional awakening to symbolic identity that projects noetic experience to a primordiality that positions the in-itself in an ontologically progressive natural condition—a transformation becomes seclusion in wholeness, and whole within its own seclusion.

While establishing a pre-condition for an awareness that accompanies an aestheticization of the lifeworld—into a compositional unification with self-identity—the conclusion to an experience of what must resonate in symbolic projection of appearances to the Self, will still perceive the observances determinable to humanity's natural ontological conceptualization.

Toward these regions of thought, originating in the transcendental realm of consciousness, self-identity posits an awareness in correspondence with an instantiation of a symbolic identity representative to the not-self, yet an essentialist feature to a radical *noesis* that is never concrete or establishes the necessary contextualization constitutive of its projection of *symbolic* identification. Through formalization of abstract subjectivity posited from a counter-position as a determinable entity composed of an objective datum—within a residuum of artefacts to self-identity that reside within certain "mental garbage" of existentiality, the certitudes of a Fichtean revolt, fall too far beyond what is envisioned the corporeal *reification* of substantiated ontological claims, subordinate to a symbolic aestheticization of the signifiers possible to interior space. Should one for a moment existentialize dialectical materialism, within the careful symbolic beauty of Lukács, into a Cartesian totalization of what had birthed *History and Class Consciousness* from a more potent aesthetic content in *The Theory of the Novel*, from the 1920s onward in Hungary, where both the Hegelian dialectic and Marxist historical materialism overshadowed vain attempts for psychoanalysis to gain a foothold upon a consciousness of the people: a world where the re-reading of Hegel were never stultified within the concepts that had birthed a psychological reification of a symbolic, Husserlian *dator* consciousness never driving philosophy into ill-repute—produced a rift between Freud and Jung; separated Freud's unconscious elevations of the Jungian Self into an analytic appropriation of its content. This perpetuated an impetus for the supply of symbolic instantiations of *being* to be generated solely through an abstraction of the inner lifeworlds of subjects' experiences through Jung—while the *imago* of those psyches blessed with symbolic experiences had been appropriated by Jungian analysts themselves. Consequentially, once the West had returned to Hegel during the 1930s, in order to reconcile with the sources of what had in essence birthed the October Revolution of 1917, somehow Western thinking were still deterred from the insights that had already become necessary, in order to diagnose the actions of the *Third Reich* before so many had been confined to camps quite unlike the ones that would likely emerge in the 21st Century, should the world project through a historical realization that any such form of confinement had not taken on an entirely new one. A form of confinement that were based in principles established by an absence of discourse, conditioned by psychoanalytic precepts that had become anti-philosophical—and biased toward the corpus of work possible of an analyst, rather than a creativity that had been historically founded by the philosophical thinkers throughout time. For the genesis of psychology itself had been generated more by Kant than any other of the 18th Century ontological philanderers. However *as* with time, human nature had always become of an alterity conditioning humanity to a self-concept, that is vulnerable to a state of resignation of compliance to a *status quo* acceptance of a discourse serving mass-appeal; and not a vitality to the human endeavor birthing the transcendence possible of a revolutionary existential conquest of the limitations in proposition of an obfuscation to a symbolization of what is total to human experience. For a potency possible to social transformation, is what propelled *Being* through its natural progression forward, as a visibility that furthered the aestheticization of a content that forms perceptions that are only features of the real world of phenomena that may be actualized throughout an acknowledgement of content reproducible to the forms for which they had stood in representation—as self-identities colliding—projecting through unconscious barriers that are particular to the confinements of a symbolic space exposed through dialectical abstraction.

If one considers the barriers existing for the coordinates of a subjective ontology to be natured by the latter, the idea that a symbolic identity is perceived by something quite invasive of primordial space, is suggestive of a delusional state—yet once it has been engaged through a totalization of the horizon as an experience never preemptive of the symbolic states of awareness, it is existential to humanity's progression through temporal space. A uniformity to the content is impossible to the totality, while remaining a presupposition to the objects that accompany manifold being from its condition, situated in the subjects copied from the internal landscape to the noetic field, where all such phenomena persist in abstract signification. The ontic field, where universality is held as a particularized conclusive appearance, to the manifold conceptions governing the projection of a self-identical, transcend their nominal boundaries becoming things-in-themselves—articulating the interior sources; never confining identity to its motile undulation as a self-regulating property of what composes the Self as a given, through which the universal remains unhindered. Though its confinement into a particular projection of a non-identical being-in-itself, modulates substance such that the factors establishing the context from which an adjudication of the laws governing symbolic space into a being-of-essence, becomes of transcendences that are posited by the mind, where there is a void of appearances as horizontal awarenesses. Such that these are formal to content, yet the form which is post-ontological and posited by the material, *noematic* objects themselves, the significations of Self never dissolve into an artificiality, or compromise of a content that resounds of a projection of this from which *animate* being is an activated analogon to the synthetic content that pre-forms ontological content from an existential horizon, where it had been abstracted into the content of an *objectively* signified space.

That the *cogito* would still operate within the guise of nothing in particular to the universality possible of an existential horizon, establishing a pre-condition for aesthetic experiences—reflexive of the possibilities in opposition to the particularism necessary of signified abstract space—self-identity's symbolic resonation is an encumbrance of the subjective will to expose Plato to the "shadows" of doubt—from where the mortal givens of Socratic *logos,* had been generated as altogether within the altruisms of a juridical dynamism; composing reality as a projection of quantum possibilities available to humanity's explorations, throughout a totality of consciousness in an ontological lifeworld.

Such that this would be a substance presupposing that being experiences an erudition proliferating through significations that are not only possible of the horizontal forms which had accompanied their appearance—yet necessitated a preemptive abstraction of all relevant content—subjectivity is self-identical and nominal to symbolic experience, projecting through a resolute and unbridled objective representability that assembles a composition of material form, into its symbolic instantiation as a qualitative encumbrance to a being-as-other. Unified through ontological relations, as a formalization of the Self throughout an actuality posited into an objective manifold self-identical, syntactical representations conform to a qualitive conceptual datum. Where we should of course become of these, such as are limitations of the transcendental *regime*, which had gone unaccompanied by an absence in self-identical representations, one would gather that the Self had gazed upon its own essence—yet reflected that the being-as-other had become of the very same. Hence, a universal co-existence is possible a modality of being, that responds to its authentication from a presupposed affirmative contextualization; while aesthetic content is more responsive to "Verneinung" [63]—in which negation and affirmation co-exist where we respond to Spinoza or Hegel's *omnes determinatio est negatio.* [64] However, it will never be upon us to supply the forms by which our own determinability would be composed of negation *stricto sensu*; it is upon us to fully recognize the possibility of signifying something that had not simply become submerged into its early morning tea, as would the empiricists of the "Mother Country" have preferred. I am more than certain that one would be resolutely, and unabashedly willing to experience a jubilation that projected toward the extremities of the commons from whence they had originated, so as to become signified into a totality of emancipatory symbolic identification—so as to compose a reality that had become particular to the heritage founding *self-identification* as a fulfilling conceptual experience mobilized by no vanities other to the Self; but those that had founded an enlightened purposiveness.

Yet, that we must transcend the oppositions to which we are indefatigably predisposed, so as to further the sense of perseverance forward—the mediating conditions identifiable as subjective compromises to the ontic content determinable to symbolic facticity, become of projections resonating through correlations with horizontal positions—justly posited as a totality of observances that conferred within the possibilities of an *a priori* composition to a material world, that is resolute within its appraisal of the pregiven constitution for which it had become an abstraction to the genus of the *forms* collective to humanity. Insofar as the structuration of the latter had become constituted by their qualitative performances of an impractical means, by which any such abstractions of reified content are those which have become subordinations to the will of humanity's common aspirations, the genesis that had modulated an aesthetic experience that is pre-ontological to the positing of what were conditioned through abstract space, becomes the noetic stratum forming an apperception of its position to Self, as the essential signification of symbolic meaning.

---

[63] A psychoanalytic principle that employs negation of an analysand(patient) in order to appropriate and evaluate the contents of their psyches. The symbolic dimension becomes particular to the analyst, while departing the consciousness of the subject that is undergoing treatment for symptoms identified as psychotic features.

[64] *Latin*: "Every determination exists as a negation".

INDEX

A

absence, vi-vii, 5, 62, 122-123, 127, 129, 131
Absolute, 15 n11
Absolutes, 6, 71
absolutes, 30, 66n
abstract, vi, 1, 46, 61, 82, 94n,108, 110, 114-115, 124-126, 129-132
abstracted, 23n, 34, 47, 75-76, 92, 131
abstracting, 6
Abstraction, 33
abstraction, iv, vi-vii, 1, 6, 8, 10-11, 19, 21-22, 30, 34, 40, 44-45, 71, 73-75nn, 81, 107, 110, 112-114, 121, 124, 129-132
abstractions, 6, 44, 46, 78, 95-96, 107, 109-110, 115, 132
abyss, 126
access, ix, 4, 28, 116-117
accessible, viii, 13, 69
accident, 106
accidental, 104
accidents, 104
accommodate, viii-ix, 98, 102, 104, 110, 127
accumulation, 95-96
achievement, vii
acquisition, 25, 27-28, 89
act, vi, ix, 12, 26-27, 43, 50, 52-53, 57, 59, 84-85, 87, 89, 99, 104-106, 114
action, iv, 6, 10-11, 13, 18, 20-21, 25, 34, 42, 52-53, 55, 57, 65, 74, 78, 81-82, 89, 123
actioned, i, 52
actions, 10, 51-52, 88, 100, 109, 117, 129
activities, i, iii, 7, 12, 83, 99, 104, 110, 112, 114, 127
activity, 11, 63, 100, 106-107, 111, 126
acts, i, vii, 9, 26, 29, 62, 66, 76, 78, 98, 103, 111-112, 127
Actualities, 59
actualities, 20, 57-58, 66-67, 73, 86, 92, 109-110, 124, 127
actuality, 2, 10-12, 18-20, 23, 28-29, 41-42, 46, 54-56, 58-60, 63-64, 73-75, 77-79, 83-85, 90, 100, 102, 123-124, 126, 131
actualization, 83
actualize, 102
actualized, iii, 130
adjudicate, iii
adjudication, 100, 108, 130
adjudications, 100
administer, 122
administered, 10, 101 n55, 118, 123
administering, iii
administrable, 2, 5, 15, 66-67, 90, 98, 101, 104-105, 109, 116-118, 123
administrate, 2, 9, 81
administrated, 4-5, 11
administrates, 26
administrating, 5
administration, 2-3, 7-9, 15-16, 83, 87
administrations, 10
administrative, 2, 8-9, 11, 14, 16-17, 25, 27-28, 99-100
administrator, 11-12
Adorno, 101 n55, 127
advancement, 61, 91

advances, 3, 28
advantage, 2, 48, 113, 117
advantages, 2
advocate, 13
aesthetic,19,21n,94, 100, 113, 115, 128-129, 131-132
aestheticization, 13, 118, 128-130
aesthetics, 113
affairs, iii, 98, 101-102, 114
affirmation, 18, 132
affirmations, 18
affirmative, 18, 131
aftermath, 13
agency, v, 9, 26, 116-117, 127
agents, 89
aggression, iii
aging, vi
agreements, 5
ailment, 52
aims, 111, 113-115
alarm, 51
algorithm, 10, 14-16
algorithmic, 61
algorithms, 10
alien, vi, viii
allowances, 102-103
altruism, v
altruisms, 131
amphiboly, 25
analogon, 131
analysand, 132 n63
analyses, 127
analysis, 114
analyst, 129, 132
analysts, 129
analytic, 25, 27, 129
analytical, 7, 44-45, 81
ancestor, 72
ancestry, 72
Ancient, 104
animals, 3
animation, 6
annihilate, 112
annihilated, v, 98
annihilation, 114
answers, 104, 109
antecedence, 78
antecedent, 5, 12, 16, 18, 20, 22, 25, 27-28, 33, 55, 58, 66, 68, 76
Anti-philosophical, 129
antinomy, 6, 19, 86
antiquated, 105, 125
antithetical, 25
apocalyptic, vi
apodicity, 84-85
apodictic, 18, 84, 86, 88
apoplexy, 118
aporetic, 119-120
aporia, 62
apotheosis, 109, 124
appeal, ix, 98, 100, 110-111, 122, 130
appealed, v, 100
appeals, 98, 100, 110, 115
appearance, 8, 12, 18-21, 57, 70, 72, 77-78, 80-81, 90, 99-100, 110, 121, 130-131
appearances,18n, 81, 98, 100-102, 110-111, 114, 123-125, 128, 130
appeared, 85, 93, 107
appearing, 114
appears, vi, viii, 43, 57, 63, 70, 95, 105
apperception, 132
apprehended, 12, 19, 46, 55, 70, 74
apprehends, 30, 67
apprehension, 10, 33, 51, 66-67, 70, 77, 122, 126
apprehensions, 22, 103
approaching, 55
appropriated, 96, 98-99, 129
appropriates, 74, 100
appropriation, i, 7, 43-44, 50, 83, 94n53-96, 112, 116, 122, 126, 129
approximately, 15
architectonic, 114
architectonically, 1
architecture, 104, 106
arena, 24, 128
Aristotelian, 9
Aristotle, 6, 25 n 20, 56 n28, 79 n38 79, 105
arms, 81, 121
artefacts, 94, 106, 129
articulations, 47, 113-114
artifice, 3-4, 15-16, 26, 35, 50, 52, 91
artifices, 115
Artificial Systems, 35
artificial, 3n, 6, 10, 14-15,(intelligence) 17n, 35,

(soul),118
artificiality, 131
artistic, vii
arts, 98, 106
Assange, Julian 27 n21
assassination, i
assemblage, 107
assemblies, 27-28
assembly, 2, 11, 14-18, 25-27, 53, 80
assertion, 34, 43, 117
assertions, viii
associated, vii, 25-28, 57-58, 67, 97, 103, 106, 117
association, 1, 4, 11, 25-26, 28, 49, 72, 85
associations, 25, 71
atmosphere, 48-49
atom, 4
atomic, 4, 24 n19
atomism, 4
atomist, 5
attempts, 10, 94, 98, 105, 107, 129
attribute, 4, 14, 28, 34-35, 42-43, 49, 79 n38, 89
attributes, 2-3n, 9, 17, 25-28, 46, 52, 69-70, 76, 84, 117
attribution, 43, 125
augmentative, 77
augmenting, 83
authentic, 82, 99, 103, 118
authentically, 125
authenticated, 1, 99, 109
authentication, 109, 118, 125, 131
authenticity, iv, 99, 107, 117, 120, 124, 126-127
authoritative, 96, 116
authorities, 27-28
automobile, 49
autonomous, 5
autonomy, 105, 120
availability, 6, 26, 81, 86, 95, 125
avarice, ii, v
awakening, vii, 122, 128
Awareness, 31
awareness, ix, 8-9, 24, 29-31, 57, 60-61, 71, 92, 96, 101, 108, 117-118, 120-121, 128, 130
awarenesses, 130

B

backfire, 2
barrier, viii
barriers, vi, 95, 104, 130
battle, 91
battles, vi
becomes, i, iv-v, 5, 11, 27-28, 44, 53, 60, 64-66, 70, 88-89, 91, 103-104, 108, 110, 116-117, 119, 121, 124, 127-128, 130, 132n
becoming, i, v, 3, 24, 28, 59, 66, 93, 96, 102, 107, 112, 115, 122-125, 128, 130
beginning, vii, 3, 6, 51
beginnings, 91, 112
behavioral, 54
Being, 6, 19, 21, 46, 59-60, 67, 74-75, 87, 99, 105, 115, 117-118, 120-121, 123-125, 128, 130
being, i, iii, viii-ix, 2-4, 6-8, 11-12, 14-15n, 17-30, 35, 42-46n, 48, 50-53, 56-62, 65-76n, 78, 80-91nn, 93-94, 99n-101, 105, 110-112, 114-118, 120-122, 124, 126-127, 129-131
Being-for-itself, 21-22,44-46,66,127; in-itself, 18 n14,21-25,35,42-46 n25, 69; in-the-world, 87-88
Beings, 29, 43
beings, 1-2, 10n, 14-19n, 22, 24-25, 42-46, 54, 57-58, 60, 67-68, 77, 80, 82, 87-88, 94-96, 108, 112-114, 118, 120, 122
belong, iii, 113, 125
belonging, 117
beneficial, 82
benefits, 47
binary, iii, 106, 120
Bio-Satellite (etc.), vi, 3 n2, 7, 13, 5 n29, 63-64, 95, 97, 101 n55
biosatellites, 3 n2

birthed, i, v, vii-viii, 113, 127, 129
birthing, 130
blossomed, 93
bodies, vii, 5, 90, 100, 103, 105
Body-politic, 111
bomb, 4
born, 2
borne, 121, 123
botanical, 55, 63
bound, 36, 56, 62, 120-121, 126
boundaries, 28, 64, 98, 119-121, 123-124, 127, 130
bravado, iv, 120
brutes, 91
bungler, 118

C

Cambridge Analytica, 27 n21
camps, 129
Canada, 115
cancel, 34, 103
cancellation, 119
capabilities, 61
capable, iii, vi-vii, 51, 63, 104, 110, 117, 127
capacities, 109, 121, 127
capacity, 69, 104
capital, 113, 127
capitalism, 122
capricious, 107, 119, 125
capture, 100, 109
captured, 93, 108
captures, 112
carbon, 49
carriers, 63, 93
carries, 90
Cartesian, 68 n32, 101, 105-106, 125, 129
casuistry, 43 n24
categorical, 84-85
categories, 8, 115
category, 2
cathode tube, 3
causal, 16, 18, 28-30, 36, 44, 48, 50-51, 53-55, 57, 66, 91, 99, 105-106, 117, 124, 126-127
Causality, 18, 51-52
causality, ii, 8 n, 22, 25, 27, 29, 31-32, 44-45, 56-57, 81, 89, 96 n, 105, 110
causation, 36, 53, 58, 79
causes, vi, 36, 80, 94, 104-105, 108-109, 124
cave, 23
centrifuge, 1
centuries, ii, x, 28, 119
Century, 20th-21st, 1-2,iii, viii-ix, 3, 9, 17, 25, 127, 129- 18th,130
certainties, 1, 5, 12, 20, 45
Certainty, 34
certainty, 8, 11-12, 18-23, 34-35, 42, 45, 57-61, 108
certitude, iii, 84
certitudes, viii, 129
challenges, 112
chamber, 121
changeable, v
changeables, 79
changed, 15, 79
changes, ix, 54, 116
changing, 32
chaotic, 53
characteristic, 56
characteristics, 78, 126
Chauvinistic, iii
chemical, 3, 50, 63, 105
chemicals, 48
choices, vi, 105, 108-110, 124
chosen, ix, 95
chronology,(genetic), 52
cinematic, 128
circulates, 16
circulation, 61-62, 88, 91
circumspections, 62
circumstance, 5, 11, 21-22, 42-43, 46, 59, 85, 91, 123
circumstances, i, v, 10, 52, 56, 85, 88, 104, 106
circumvention, 57-59, 61-62, 67
citizen, v, 53, 122
citizenry, 91
citizens, 66, 91
civil, 85, 89, 91
civilization, vi, 50
civilizations, viii
civilized, 64
claims, 118, 129
classification, vii, 8

classifications, 1, 7-8, 29 classified, 2, 10, 48, 61
classifies, 2
classless, 113
climate, 94
clouds, *a mode of nature*, 55-56

coalesce,(proxy objects), 12
coalescence, 29, 55, 57, 83 coalescent, 83 coalition,(value), 27 code,(data identities) 10-11
Coerce, 86 coercion, 87 Coercive superstructures, 7, 85 cogitation, 29
cogitations, 14
cogitative, 43
Cogitatively, 57
cogitatively, 34
Cogito, 27, 101

cogito, 18n, 88n, 106, 114, 116, 120, 131
cognition, 14, 22, 34, 54
cognitions, 6
cognitive, 48, 118, 120-121
coherence, 79, 126
coincidences, 119
collateralized, 59
collective, v, vii-viii, 5-8, 10, 14-16, 19-20, 23-24, 26, 29, 35, 42-45, 60-62, 70-71, 80-81, 83n-92, 94-95, 104-105, 108-109, 111, 116-117, 119, 125, 132

collectively, 19, 43, 64, 88
collectives, iv, viii, 3, 8-9, 14, 19, 23n, 26, 28, 42-43, 45, 88, 93
Collectivity, 80

collectivity, 1-2, 5, 7, 10-11, 14-15, 19-20, 24-27, 35, 42, 53, 57, 60, 64, 69-70, 80-81, 83, 85, 87, 90
collectivization, 2, 61-62, 66, 91

collectivized, 2, 88
collects, 121
collide, 50, 57
colliding, 130
collusion, v, 100
colors, 78
combination, 49, 53, 55, 78-79, 119
commensurate, 5, 25, 85-86
commerce, 7, 9, 11, 64-65
commercial, 5, 11, 101
commodification, 59
commodity, ii, vi, 8, 11, 122
commonality, 16-17, 66
commonplace, 96, 103
commons (totality),132
communications, 67
communion, 111
communities, vi, 23, 90
compliance, ii, 80, 130
complications, 106
comply,(w/ objectivi-ty) 117
component, v, vii, 26, 50, 79, 82, 96, 99, 103, 112, 116, 119, 128
components, iv, 12, 67, 83, 99, 105
compose, 101, 108, 115, 120, 132
composed, 94n, 110, 118, 122, 125, 129, 132
composes, 34, 84n, 107-108, 121, 130
composing, 106, 110, 120, 131
composite, 17, 30, 105
composition, 9n, 87, 94, 96-97, 102, 104-105, 107-109, 114-115, 118-119, 121, 131-132
compositional, 128
compositions, 107, 115, 117
compound, 49-50, 63
compounding, ix
comprehensible, 94, 113
comprehension, 115
comprehensive, iii

compromised, 66
compromises, vii, 109, 117, 132
compulsory, 53, 86
computer, 1, 4-6, 9-10, 14-15
computers, 2, 4
conceivable, 8, 87, 126
conceive, viii, 13, 104
conceived, i, 70-71, 94, 99, 123, 128
Concept, 45
concept, i, v, vii-ix, 3, 6-7n, 10-15nn, 18n, 20-25nn, 43n, 56n,62-66n,69n,79n, 82n, 88n, 93, 96n, 101n-102, 107, 116, 119-121, 124n, 126, 130
conception, 7, 10, 14-15, 17, 21n-25, 27, 30n, 34-36, 40, 42-44, 50, 62-63, 69, 71-72, 74-75, 77, 80-82, 87-88, 95, 109, 123
conceptionist, 8
conceptions, 7, 9, 18, 24-25, 36, 42-44, 46, 65, 69, 72, 82, 123, 130
concepts, iii, v, vii, 6, 94-95, 98, 101, 106, 109, 111, 114, 125, 129
conceptual, 17n, 27, 47, 71, 95, 99, 102, 110, 126, 128, 131-132
conceptualization, 128
conceptualize, 102
conceptualized, 44
conclusions, viii, 36, 44, 91, 104
concrete, vii, 97, 112, 126, 129
concretion, 84-86
concurrent, 11, 18, 28, 67, 69, 71, 73, 75-76, 78, 80, 82
Conditional, 18, 73-74
conditional, 5, 12, 15-26, 28-29, 40, 42-46, 48, 51, 57-60, 62, 69-70, 72, 74-76, 78, 81, 83, 101
conditionalities, 80, 83
Conditionality, 72
conditionality, 24, 55-56, 58-60, 73-78, 81-83
conditionally, 26, 58
conditioned, v, viii, 23, 25, 40-41, 44-46, 66, 71-72, 92, 99, 110, 112, 124, 129, 132
conditioning, 83, 130
Conditions, 41
conditions, ii, vii-ix, 1-2, 8-9, 11-12, 14, 16-21, 23, 25-26, 28-30, 33, 35-36, 38, 41-46, 48, 50-52, 55-61, 66-67, 69-76, 78, 80-82, 84-87, 96, 98, 100, 102-104, 108-109, 112, 116-117, 121-126, 128, 132
conduct, i, iv, 53, 64, 76, 95, 98, 103, 106-109
configuration, 11, 15, 24, 26-28, 30, 52-53
configurations, 17, 30
confinement, 129-130
conflict, 28
conflicts, 67, 116
conform, 131
conforming, v
confrontation, 107, 109-110
confronted, 116-117
confused, 3, 108
confusion, 29, 119-120
congenital, 52
connectedness, 4, 9, 59, 80-81
connecting, 62
connection, ii, iv, 3n, 49, 63, 69, 86-88, 124
connectivity, 62
conquest, 84, 130
conquests, 105, 109
conscious, 69, 94, 99, 101, 126
Consciousness, 129
consciousness, 1, 4, 6, 8, 11-13, 15n -17,

19, 23 n, 28-29, 35, 40, 49, 52-53, 59 n-62 n, 65-67, 69-71, 74 n, 83, 87, 89 n -91, 96, 98, 100-102, 104, 106-109, 115, 120-121, 128-129, 131-132 n
consciousnesses, 106
consensus, 2
consent, 1, 83
consequence, 59
consequences, 118
consequential, 13, 101, 115-116, 125, 127
consequentialism, 56
consolidation, 121
constellated, 108
constellation, 101
constellations, 15, 126
constitute, 56, 70, 84-86, 89, 91, 125
constituted, 30, 43, 75, 84, 88, 91, 99, 123, 125-127, 132
constitutes, 14, 25, 60, 87, 95
constituting, 43, 84
constitution, 17, 85-88, 90-91, 115, 132
constitutional, 90, 99
constitutions, 90
constitutive, 56, 75, 84-87, 89-91, 101, 109, 114, 121-124, 126-129
construct, 122
constructed, 120, 128
construction, 79
consume, vii, 127
consumed, iv, 95, 99
consumeristic, 127
consumers, vii, 99
consumes, i
consumption, iv, 99, 122
consumptive, 67, 127
contained, vii, 4, 6, 10, 15-16, 18, 25-30, 50, 60, 66, 100, 105, 117
containing, 8-9, 36
containments, 9, 26-27, 30
contemplation, 5, 56, 104, 108, 112, 114
contemplative, 107, 112
contemporalities, 73, 78
contemporaneity, 25, 67, 70, 73-74, 76, 78, 81
Contemporaneous, 17, 73
contemporaneous, 1, 4, 22-26, 28, 33, 43, 45-46, 49, 56-57, 63, 66-67, 69-70, 72-78, 81
contemporaneously, 12, 17, 21, 35, 70, 73, 78
contemporarian, 84
Contemporary, ii, iv, vi, viii, x, 2, 4, 6, 8, 10, 12, 16, 18, 20, 22, 24, 26, 28, 30, 32, 34, 36, 38, 40, 42, 44, 46, 50, 52, 54, 56, 58, 60, 62, 64, 66, 68, 70, 72, 74, 76, 78, 80, 82, 84, 86, 88, 90, 92, 94, 96, 100, 102, 104, 106, 108, 110, 112, 114, 116, 118, 120, 122, 124, 126, 128, 130, 132
contemporary, 1, 4-5, 7, 24-25, 27, 50, 62, 66-67, 71-73, 75, 78, 81-83, 86
content, i-ii, vi-viii, 1, 5-6, 8, 10, 12-14, 18-26, 28-29, 31, 33-35, 40-43n, 45-47, 55-63n, 67, 71, 80-81, 83, 98, 100, 107, 109-110, 112, 114, 116, 118, 120, 122, 124, 126-132
context, 13, 46, 59, 86, 91, 95, 106-108, 110-112, 114-118, 122-123, 128, 130
contexts, 57
contextualization, 129, 131
contiguous, 17, 25-27, 30, 45, 57-58, 65, 69, 71, 75, 95

continent, vii
continental, vii
continents, 48
Contingencies, 60, 73-74
contingencies, 12, 18-20, 27-29, 45, 57-60, 62-63, 68, 73-75, 77-78, 83, 86
contingency, 8, 11-12, 15, 17-21, 24, 27-29, 35, 41, 43, 46, 57-61, 63, 73-77, 80-81, 83
Contingent, 41, 60
contingent, 5, 9, 11-12, 15, 17-24, 27, 41, 43-48, 52, 57-58, 61-63, 65, 67, 70-71, 73-77, 80-81, 83, 86, 100, 114
contingents, 25-27, 30, 57, 83
Continuum Publishing, 101 n55
contradiction, 7, 10, 44, 65, 83-85
contradictions, 87, 89, 119
contradictory, 27
contraries, 34
contrariness, 17, 33, 57-58
controlled, 96, 105, 112, 128
controlling, vii, 2
controls, 6, 53, 94, 116
convenience, 48, 54,65
convention, 81
conventions, 10, 13
converts, 48
conveyance, 12, 15, 29, 35, 61
conveyances, 6
coordinates, 10, 92-93, 95, 100, 111, 113-114, 116, 120, 122-124, 126, 130
corporate, 3, 5, 25, 54, 64, 82-83, 91
corporations, vii
Corporatist, 82
corporatist, 81-82
corporeal, 3, 89, 121, 125, 129
corpus, 129
correlation, 11, 29, 48
correlations, 132
correlative, 54
correspond, 4, 11, 78
correspondence, 106, 111, 114-115, 124, 128
correspondent, 38
corresponds, 3, 12, 81, 112
corridors, iii
corroborative, 72
corruption, 16
cosmic, 3
countries, ix
courts, iv
cranium, 119
creative, 94
creativity, vii, 129
creature, iii
creatures, ii, 63, 94-95, 112
criminal, 87
criminals, 113
crippling, 6
crises, 122
Crisis of the European Sciences, 116
crisis, viii
critical, 11, 71, 120, 127
Critique of Pure Reason, 20
Cross-referencing, 14
crossroads, 125
crush, vi
crushing, 43
cubists, 127
cultural, ii, vii, 1-3, 5, 7-9, 16, 25, 28-29, 51, 53, 57-58, 64-67, 70, 81, 90, 92, 99, 118
culturalism, 1
culture, vi, 1-2, 7-8, 51-54, 65-66, 81, 91, 94-95, 125, 127
cultures, 2, 51-52, 71
currencies, 9
currency, i, 1, 5, 8, 10-11, 26, 30, 59, 64-66, 89-91, 93

D

daily, 53-54, 64-65
damage, vi, 89
damages, iii
darkness, ix, 118, 126
Darwinian, 112
Darwinism, 88
Dasein, 86 n46, 87-89
Data Absolute, 15n-16

data, 8-10, 12, 14-15, 17, 25-28, 69
Data-information, 27
Dator consciousness, 129
datum, 27, 110, 129, 131
deadlock, 112, 124
debts, iii, vi, 29
decades, ii, ix, 17
decay, 70, 98
decaying, 4
deceived, 119
deception, 10, 43
deconstruct, 88
deeper, 50, 104
defeat, 118
degenerating, ix
degeneration, 125
degradation, 66
deification, 125
Deleuze, 89 n49
deliverance, 59
delivered, i, vi-vii, 2, 27, 101
delivering, 62
delivers, 103, 105
delusional, 130
delusive, 120, 123
democracy, iii, 2
democratic, 1-2
denominational, 52
dentist, 112
departure, 108, 111
depicted, i, viii, 2, 58, 113, 118
deposing, 99
deprived, 66, 117
Descartes, 125
designs, 54, 62, 65, 121, 126
desirable, 7
desire, 67
desired, vii, 67, 88, 103, 114
despotic, 91, 123
despotism, 125
destined, iii, 112
destinies, 107
destroy, vi, 53
destroyed, 53
destroying, 2
destroys, 50
destructive, vi, 29, 53
detachable, 124
determinability, 100, 126, 132
determinable, 95, 109, 115-120, 123, 128-129, 132
determinate, 86
determinateness, 19, 22, 36, 56-58, 60-61, 64-65, 72, 83, 85-86, 88, 90
determination, ix, 22, 126, 132
determinations, 36, 84-89, 100, 123, 125
determine, vii, 3, 9, 109
determining, 13, 104, 117, 120
developed, 54, 94, 104, 112, 114, 119
developing, i
development, ii, viii, 66, 102, 104, 113, 118
developmental, 4, 17, 52
developments, 3-4, 13, 95-96, 106, 113
device, 18, 54
devices, 3, 9, 54, 81
devolution, 66
devouring, v
diachronic, 103
diachronically, 104
diachrony, 71
diagnosable, x, 13, 115, 118, 122
diagnose, 129
Diagram, 40
Dialectic of Enlightenment, 127
dialectic, 62n, 86, 102, 119, 129
dialectical, iii, ix, 5-6, 46n, 105-107, 110-111, 113-116, 119, 122-123, 127-130
dialectically, 94, 109, 115, 125
Dialectics, 101n
dichotomy, 1, 28
differences, 93, 116
different, 5, 21, 77, 79
differentia, 6, 34, 57-58, 78
differential, 21, 58, 104
differentiates, ix
digital-space 3 n,17 n
Dimension, 98
dimension, 103n-112, 114-115, 117-120, (symbolic),132 n63
dimensional, 10, 111, 121

dimensions, 98, 105, 109
dinosaurs, 64
directive, 1, 4, 9, 17, 66
disassembles, 19, 54
disasters, vi, 95
disavowal, 93
disavowed, 119
disciplines, 106
disclose, 46
disclosed, 75, 88
disclosedness, 88
discloses, 20, 34, 43, 82, 121
disclosure, 17, 23, 44, 99, 103, 107
discourse, iii-iv, viii-ix, 94, 98-99, 106-107, 113, 129-130
discoveries, 106
discredited, 118
disease, 52, 65, 90
disintegration, 100
dispossessed, v
disrepair, ii, iv, vi, 93
dissimilar, 49, 61, 66, 77-78
dissociation, 95
dissolution, vi, 100
dissolve, 131
dissolved, 123
dissolves, 98, 120
dissolving, vi
distantiated, 94, 122, 127
distortions, 113
distracted, ix
distractions, 99
distribute, 110
distributed, 118
distributes, 25
distribution, 5, 14-16, 62, 64, 86
distributiva communitiva, 85
distributive, 98, 116
disunity, iii, vi
divided, 4, 118
divine, 84, 111
division, 4
doctrines, 120
dogmatic, 65
doing, 87
domain, 103n, 114, 124
domestic, 48
dominated, ii, 94, 127
dominates, 125
dominating, iii
dominion, 117
doubts, 93, 98, 107
dreams, vii, 94
driven, i-ii, iv-vi, 5, 54, 63, 65, 99, 105, 109, 123
duality, 56, 105-106
duration, 13
duties, 6, 85
dutiful, vii
duty, 85, 89
dynamic, 24, 55, 58
Dynamical, 22
dynamical, 11, 25-26, 51, 56-58, 61-62, 64, 66, 70-71, 80, 87, 110
dynamically, 22, 57, 67, 70, 81
dynamics, 3, 9, 11-12, 53, 58, 60, 62, 64-65, 81
dynamism, 131
dystopian, 100

E

Earth, v, viii, 3n-4, 15n, 91, 96
earth, 48, 105
echoing, iii, 93
eclipse, 127
ecological, 51, 64
economic, ii, 3 n2, 83-84, 87, 89-91, 94, 104, 106-107, 112-113, 116-117, 127
economical, 64
economies, viii
economized, 84
ecosystem, 50, 56, 62-63
ecosystems, 51
Écrits, 103 n56
ecstasis, 87
ecstatical, 87
edification, vi, 64
edifices, i
edificial, 102, 104
edified, 17, 28
edify, 29
effects, 3n, 6, 18, 32, 36, 45, 50, 54-57, 66, 79-80, 127
effectual, 55, 79-81, 98
efficiency, 54
efficient, vi
effort, vii, 8
efforts, 8, 103, 127
ego, 84, 86, 88 n47, 101-103 n86, 109,

112, 122, 124-125
egos, 84 n42
eidos,3 n,79 n
electoral, iii
electorate, 105
electro-magnetic field, 4
electrons, 4
element, 1, 48-49, 55-56, 62
elemental, 49, 79
elements, 5, 12, 22, 30, 32, 48, 55-56, 62-63, 79, 105
elevations, 129
elite, elites (cultural)vii, 3
elucidation, 8
Elucidations, ii, iv, vi, viii, x, 2, 4, 6, 8, 10, 12, 16, 18, 20, 22, 24, 26, 28, 30, 32, 34, 36, 38, 40, 42, 44, 46, 50, 52, 54, 56, 58, 60, 62, 64, 66, 68, 70, 72, 74, 76, 78, 80, 82, 84, 86, 88, 90, 92, 94, 96, 100, 102, 104, 106, 108, 110, 112, 114, 116, 118, 120, 122, 124, 126, 128, 130, 132
emancipated, 106, 117
emancipation, 96, 100
emancipatory, ii, vii, 7n, 99n, 102, 106, 112-113, 116-117, 132
embattlement, iii
embodied, v, 93, 119
embodiment, 99
embody, vii
embracing, 87
embryonic, ii
emerge, 127, 129
emerged, x, 3, 13, 46, 105, 123-124
emergency, 49
emergent, 91
emerging, vi
emotionality, 53, 57
empirical, 22, 55, 82, 109
empirically, 22
Empiricism, 82
empiricism, 82
empiricists, 132
employment, 48
empowered, 62
encrypted, 15
encumbrance, 131
encumbrances, 93
endangered, 51
endangerment, 51, 63, 98
endangers, 65
endeavor, vii, 6, 8, 10, 102, 114, 119, 130
endeavored, 9, 94
endeavors, 6, 95, 97-98, 109
ending, 93-94
enemies, 118
enemy, 87, 113
energeia, 101
energies, 55, 94, 96
energy(fossil fuels), 64
engaged, 62, 96, 130
engagement, 113
engages, 87, 103
engineering, 104
engines, 48
enjoyment, 65
enlightened, 128, 132
Enlightenment, 5, 127
enlightenment, 113
enterprise, viii, 59, 96, 101, 124
enterprises, 114, 123, 128
enterprising, 105
entertainment, 2
entities, 9, 82, 84, 122
entitled, 63
entity, 3, 5, 59, 64, 67, 126, 129
environmental, 77
envisioned, 99, 129
epiphanical,(revelation), 72
epistemological, 21, 35, 120
epistemology, 25
epochal, 1
epochs, 71
equality, iii
equanimity, 19, 52
equation, 66
equations, 50
equipment, 4, 54
equiprimordial, 91n
erudition, 131
escape, iii, 43, 53, 98, 126
escapes, 6, 63
escaping, v, 106
eschatological, 72, 107, 111

espionage, 1
essence, i,6n,12,15n, 25-30, 47, 50, 54, 64, 66-67, 77, 84-88n, 90-91, 95, 99,101n, 111, 121, 129-131
essences, 52,55n, 58, 84, 90, 106
essential, vi, 5, 7, 17, 26, 28, 49, 51, 59, 62, 67, 74, 79, 86-87, 103, 132
essentialist, 99, 123, 128
essentiality, 65
essentialness, 86
establishing, 114, 123, 128, 130-131
establishment, ii, 2, 13, 125
estranged, 125
eternal, 89, 110
eternity, 59
ether, 126
ethic, 83
ethical, 65-66, 81, 84-85, 87-88, 102, 107, 111-113
Ethics, 25
ethics, 12, 84
etymological, 12
etymologically, 58
etymology, 19
European, The Crisis of “”sciences, 116
evaporate, 48, 126
eventism, 105-107
events, ix, 1-2, 4, 25, 30, 50-51, 53, 56, 71, 92, 102, 104-105, 124
Everything, 25, 59
everything, vii, 10, 48, 53, 59
evil, 91, 113
evils, 102, 105
evolution, *-natural* ii, *-human* v, 99, *-personal*, 66, *of ideas*, 106
evolutional, 63
evolutionary, 13, 51
evolutions, 66
evolve, 2, 30, 92
evolved, viii-ix, 2, 52, 54
evolving, 17, 51
exaltation, v
excellence, iii
exclude, 120
excluded, 43, 117
exclusion, i-iii
exclusions, iii, viii
exclusivity, 98
excursion, 111
excursions, iv
exigencies, 105
existed, 71
existences, v, viii, 111, 128
existent, 2, 27, 30, 45, 55, 68, 70, 81, 128,
existential, v-vi, 30,66, 82, 87, 92, 96,107-109, 115-116, 120, 125-128, 130-131
existentiality, 107, 129
existentialization, 116 n
existentialize, 129
existentialized, 116 n
existents, 66, 68, 78
existenz, 99
existing, 16, 45, 54-55, 81, 89, 120, 130
exists, iv, viii, 36-37, 48, 54, 87, 132
expanding, 71
expectancy, 59
expectations, 94-95
experiences, 2, 89, 96 n53, 103, 105, 108-109, 111, 123, 129, 131
experiments, 4
exploited, 122
exploration, 13
explorations, 59, 94, 131
explore, 12
explosion, 4
explosive, 53
exponential, 105
exponentially, 105
exponents, 107, 122
exposé, 27 n21
exposed, iv, 104, 107, 121, 130
exposes, ii, 108
exposition, 96, 115
extended, 84-85
extending, 85
extension, 7, 125
extensions, 28 n22, 93, 96, 107, 123
exterior, 18-19, 49, 56-57, 67
exteriority, 8, 12, 16, 20, 33, 35, 58
external, 120

externally, 101
extinction, 64
extreme, 50, 54, 90
extremities, 132
eyes, ix

F

fabricated, 54
fabrication, 4, 11, 58, 67
fabrications, 2, 67
Facebook, 27 n21
facilitate, 54
facilitated, 54, 62, 95
facility, 54
facticity, 6, 11, 17, 29-30, 62,66n, 71, 82, 88-89, 132
faction, 96

factions, vii, 8, 64, 98, 116
factors, 123, 130
facts, 71
factual, 15, 29, 90
faculties, 62, 111
faculty, 12, 24, 34
faith, 102
falling, 88n-89, 94
falsified, 68
falsities, iv
fantasies, 102

fashion, 103, 114
fashions, 30
fate, 82, 103
fates, 89
faults, 119
features, 125, 130, 132
federal, 27
feeling, iii
fellowship, 53, 110
female, iii
femininity, ii-iii
ferocity, 53
Feuerbach, 94 n51
Fichte, 104, 114, 126
Fichtean, 129
fictions, 123

fictitious, vii, 59
fifties, *nineteen-*, 4
filiation, vii, 17, 49, 82, 92, 95-96, 105, 107, 119-120
films, 1
finite, 23-24, 36, 44, 60, 71-73, 75, 78
finitude, 24, 52, 61, 71-74, 78, 120
firewall, 9
fission, 4

fixations, 127
flames, 104
flash, 5
flowing, 10
flux, iv, 77, 79-80, 101
fluxion, 102
forces, iv, viii, 43, 53, 57, 105-106, 112
foretell, 112
for-itself, *being-in-and-*, 127
formal, 88, 99-100, 107, 117, 131
formalization, 95, 97, 101-102, 108, 119, 123-124, 128-129, 131
formalizations, 128
formalize, 103
formalized, 111
formalizes, 123
formation, 3, 50, 94, 101-102, 110, 112, 120, 122, 124-125
formative, 84
forming, 70, 80, 89, 127, 132

forms, i-ii, iv-v, 3, 22, 25n, 29, 36, 38, 42, 46-47, 51-52, 61-63, 67, 69, 83, 90, 92, 95, 100-102, 105n, 107-110, 115, 118-119, 123-125, 127-128, 130-132
forties, *nineteen-* , ix
forum, 80
Fossil fuels, 48n-49, 64
fought, ii-iii
found, 3, 5-9, 11, 13, 17, 23, 25-26, 29, 34-35, 51, 55, 65-67, 78, 80, 83, 98, 102, 113
foundation, 7, 24
founded, 1, 27, 78, 96, 109, 123, 129, 132
founder, 27
founding, 132

fragility, 118
fragmentary, 121
frailties, 108, 118
framed, 14, 59, 123
framework, viii, 113-114, 127-128
framing, 114
freedom, 52-53, 66-67, 95-96, 113
freedoms, 51, 66, 96,

99, 116-117
French, 115
Freud, 18 n14, 118
n61, 129
Freudian, 96
n53, frontiers,
iv, viii fruition,
iv fruits, vi, 94
fuel, 6, 49
fuels, 48n-49, 64
fulfilment, 124
functionality, 9,
14-15, 35, 54-56,
66
fundamental, 51, 90
furnaces, 48 *see* n26
fused, 58, 120
fusion, 98
futurist, 2, 20

G

galaxies, 3
gaseous, 48
gaze, 96, 99, 101,
113, 118, 127
gazes, 121
gender, iii
genera, 19, 25-28,
51-52, 69-70, 105
generalities, 82
Generality, 42

generality, 1, 5, 7,
10, 19, 26, 42-43,
62, 69, 80-81, 83
generalized, 28
generate, 50, 100,
111, 114
generated, 6, 12 n9, 22,
51-52, 98, 101,
105-107, 111,

113, 127-129, 131

generates, 51
generation, iv, 25,
52, 105
generations, v,
94-95, 106
generative, 51-52,
70, 97, 107
genesis, v, 13, 25,
100, 102, 107,
129, 132
genetic, 3, 52, 88
genetically, 95
Genus, 6, 10-11, 19,
22, 25, 30, 32-33,
51-53, 65, 72, 82
genus, 30, 70, 89,
105, 132
Geo-science, 84
geographical, 10
geographically, 8
geography, 27
geologically, 48
German, 91 n50
gifts, 118, 123
givenness, 87, 118
givens, 117, 123, 131
glimpse, ii, vii, 99,
101, 121, 126
glimpsed, 98
glimpses, 64
global, vi, viii-ix, 4,

53, 92, 101, 112,
122
globe, v
goal, 49, 102
goals, iv
governance, 8-9, 64,
90
governances, 121
governed, 65, 96

governing, iii, 92,

114, 130
government, 26, 90
governmental, 27, 83
governments, 9
greater, viii, 3, 8, 51,
53-54, 56, 64-66,
82, 90, 94, 106,
113, 118, 127
greed, 112
grounding, 111
grounds, 20
groups, viii, 1, 7,
64-65
Grund, 91 n50
guardianship, 127
guidance, 84, 123
guiding, 101

H

habitat, 51
habitats, 51
hacker, 11
happening, 112
happiness, v
haunt, 119
heads, 103
heal, 54
healthier, 89
heated, 48
heavens, 111
Hegel, 3 n, 10, 14,
18 n,
30 n, 43 n, 47, 74 n,75,
101, 119, 121,
125, 129, 132
Hegelian,7, 43, 46,
62, 82, 88 n, 102,
125, 129
hegemonic, 102
hegemonizes, 83
Heidegger, 87 n46,
91 n50
Heideggerian, 15
n10
88 n47, 99, 121

Heraclitus, 79
heritage, 132
hermeneutical, 10, 19
hermeneutically, 119
hierarchical, 7
hierarchies, 2
higher, vii, 51, 91, 107, 113
historic, 4
historical, ii, vi, 64, 71-72, 84-86, 106, 111, 120, 129
historically, 109-110, 129
Historicity, 37-38, 71
historicity, 10, 38, 67, 71-72
histories, 108
Hobbesian, 125
holism, 4
homes, 14, 48
hopes, i, vii, 93
horizon, i-ii, v, viii-ix, 2, 25 n, 44, 78, 80, 84-87 n, 92-94, 96-99, 101, 103 n, 105, 112-113, 121, 124 n, 126, 128, 130-131
horizons, 36,46,62n 86n,95n-98, 100, 106-107, 114, 122, 127
horizontal, 47, 101, 110, 115-116, 127-128, 130-132
Horkheimer, 127
host, 9, 17, 26-28
hosts, 27
household, 48
human, i-vii, ix, 1-16nn, 18, 24, 26, 30, 33, 46, 48n, 50-54, 62-63, 66n, 69n, 84n, 89, 91, 94n-97n, 102, 105, 107, 112, 117, 119, 123, 126, 130
humanists, vii
Humanity, i
humanity, viii-ix, 15-16n,28n, 30, 51, 53-54, 62, 71, 89n, 94n-95, 100-101, 107, 112, 118, 122, 125-126, 128, 130-132
Humankind, 30
humankind, ii, v, ix, 93-95, 99, 105-106, 109, 111-113, 118, 125
Human-made, 48
humanoid, 96
humans, 4, 12, 29, 52, 54, 61, 94
Hungary, 129
hunted, 63
hunter, 63
hunts, 63
Hurricane Eddy, 29 (*the 6 O' Clock news*)

Husserl, 18, 43, n 68, 82, 87-89, 102, 114, 116
Husserlian, 129
hydrocarbon, 48
hydrogen, 49
hyper-sexuality, 102

I

Iceland, 27 n21
iconoclastic, 1, 83
iconoclasts, 1, 7
Idealism, 69, 83
idealism, 83, 85, 87
idealist, 43
ideality, 6, 19
ideals, 113, 118
ideas, iv-v, vii, 13, 30, 55-56, 67, 93, 98, 106-107, 120
ideation, 24, 30, 70, 115

identical, ii, iv, 8,11, 69-70, 83-91, 93, 95-96, 98-99, 109-111, 116-117, 119-122, 130-131
identicals, 85
identical Self, 109-110
identifiability, 118
Identifiable, 3
identifiable, ii, v-vi, viii, 23-24, 51, 71, 95, 103, 105, 110, 117, 122, 124, 126, 132
identifiably, 58
identification,7n,23n, 72, 86, 99n, 104, 108, 111, 114, 120-121, 124, 129, 132
identified, 9, 15, 22, 52-53, 69, 86, 108, 111, 115, 132
identifies, 3, 7, 9, 22, 48, 53, 56, 60, 68, 72, 77, 82, 104,

106
identifying, 49, 56, 89, 94, 103
identities, iii-iv, vii, 7, 11, 14, 109, 113, 126, 130
identity, iii-v, 1, 9-10, 43, 47, 79n, 96, 99n, 102, 109-112, 115-117, 121-124n, 126-128, 130-131
ideological, 83
ideologies, 82
idiosyncrasies, 120
idiosyncrasy, 60
idiot, 2
ignorance, ii, viii, 100
ill-mannered, 99
illness, 87, 91
illuminated, 63
illuminates, 110
illuminating, 126
illumination, ix, 63, 112, 121
illusory, 107, 110, 120
image, 3, 10, 12, 15, 18, 20-21, 23-24, 35, 40, 42-46, 60, 75-78, 95, 105, 112, 128
Image-representation, 21
Image-representations, 76
Images, 60
Images-in-representation, 15, 17, 24-25, 29, 43-44, 77-78, (alone) 106, 111, 118, 121, 123
imagination, i-ii, vii, 7-8, 54, 63, 106, 109, 123
imagined, 65, 126, 128
imaginings, 105
imago, 103, 129
imbalances, 117
immanence, 78, 125
immanent, x, 125
immaterial, v, 64
immediacies, iii, 115
immediacy, 51, 57, 61, 84
immediate, iv, 1, 25, 38, 49, 63, 111
imperative, 1-2, 7, 84-85, 87, 117
imperatives, ii, 90
imperfection, 54
impossibilities, 6
impossibility, ix, 62n, 71, 114, 118, 120
impossible, ii, vi, 130
inauthentic, 99
inauthenticity, 102
incarnations, 97, 102
inception, 94
inclusion, 20
inclusions, 98
inclusive, ii, 66
incoherence, 53
incomplete, iv
indebtedness, 11, 29, 64, 80
independence, 94
independent, 7, 14-15, 21, 37, 47, 89, 94, 106
individualities, 97
individuality, 101, 116
individuals, v, viii, 3, 5-7, 64, 100, 113, 116
individuated, iii, 1, 16, 64, 68, 80, 82, 99 n54, 117
individuation, 7 n4, 118 n61

industrial, 106, 112-113, 118, 122
industrialization, 3
inequality, v
inequity, 107, 123
inertia, 61
inertial, 62
inferiority, 111
infiltrating, 11
infinite, 15n, 23-24, 36, 41-42, 44-46, 59-62, 70-78, 80, 84-86, 125
infinitely, 23, 41, 75, 77, 98
infinitude, 44, 72
Infinity, 41
infinity, 6, 8, 10, 14, 16, 36, 41, 44, 59-60, 71, 73, 76, 80, 85, 87
influence, 7, 18-19, 27, 52, 58-61, 66-67
influenced, 4
influences, 9, 58
influencing, vii
Information, 28
information, vi, 6, 8-10, 14-18,

25-30, 62-63, 69-71, 82-83, 100
informational, 17, 28-30, 66, 70
informed, viii-ix, 63, 99
infrastructure, vii
infrastructures, 51
inhabit, 13
inhabitants, ii
inhabited, 123, 126
inherence, 29, 57-58
Inherent contradiction 7, -*purposiveness* 17,-*system,* 26 -*merge* 28, 53, 55, 61, 83, 87, 100, 119
inherently, 115
inheritance, 65, 71
inherited, 5, 118
inheritor, 88
inheritors, 13
inhuman, 94
in-itself, 20-25, 34, 42, 44-45, 82, 112, 120
injustice, i
injustices, v
inner, vi, viii, 10, 20, 93, 100, 102, 109-110, 112, 116, 121, 129
innocence, iv, 53
input, iii, *in-representation*, 23-24, 45, 76, 78
insight, iii, 96
insights, 6, 109, 129
instance, 10, 29, 43, 45, 49, 55, 102, 104, 106, 127
instantiated, 6, 75, 95, 97, 99, 109, 111, 115, 117, 120, 122, 126
Instantiates a *logos* identifiable to *Being*, 124
instantiating, 102
instantiation,75n, 89n, 99, 101, 103n, 107, 115, 121, 124, 127-128, 131
instantiations, 118, 129
instinct, 112
instincts, 105
instinctual, 94, 112, 118
instinctually, 63
instituted, vii
institutional, 93
institutionalized, 8
institutions, iii, 101, 122
instructions, 5, 16
instrumental, 19, 64, 82, 102
instrumentalizes, 83
instrumentation, 9, 61, 83
instruments, 2-3, 6, 10, 14, 22, 34, 48, 66, 81, 110
insular, vii
intellect, 4-5, 113, 123
intellection, 108, 113, 115
intellects, 111
intellectual, viii, 5
intelligence, 1, 17
intelligences, viii
intelligentsia, 125
intelligibility, 122
intelligible, 116, 121
intentionalities, 88
intentionality, 15-16, 66, 88, (*object of intersubjectivity*)

interaction, 11-12, 48
interactions, 53, 96
interactive, 30
interacts, 25, 49, 51
interchange, 27
interconnected, 16n
interconnectedness, 16, 51, 62, 81
intercourse, 19
interests, 85, 100-101, 111
interfere, 103
interference, 7
interferences, 53
interfering, 51
interior, 16, 18, 114, 129-130
interiority, 78, 83
interlinked, 28 n22
interminable, 50
intermingle, 62
internal, 3, 9, 103, 105, 107, 109, 116, 130
internalization, 123
internet, 9 n6, 29
interplay, 20, 27, 44, 57, 102, 124
interpret, 52
interpretation, 79
interpreted, 52, 67, 119
intersection, 97
intersects, 125
interstices, v, 116
intersubjective, 83-88 n, 119, 121,

124 n62
intersubjectively, 89, 114
intersubjectivity, 86-87, 123
intertwined, 3, 51, 118
intervention, 15
in-themselves, 18, 22, 24, 42-43, 45-46, 84
intuition, 45, 48, 63
intuitional, 30
intuitions, 5, 22, 38, 55
invention, 2
inventions, 13
inversion, 102
inverted, 22, 73
investigation, 44, 49
investment, 64
invisibility, 96
invisible, 96, 101n, 122
involuntarily, 120
involuntary, 12
involved, 12, 54, 94
involvement, viii, 90, 110
involvements, ix
irreconcilable(value), 64
irreducible, 98
irrefutable, 110

J

Japan, 4
Japanese, 4
jeopardization, 51
jeopardize, 89, 113
jeopardized, 47
jeopardizing, 89
jeopardy, 63
jet, 48
jouissance, 102
joy, 95, 122-123
jubilation, 132
judgements, 110
judgment, ix, 8, 20, 22-23, 43-45, 56, 81, 102, 115
judgments, 3, 7, 20, 23, 45-46, 67, 72, 81, 83, 111, 116
Jung, 129
Jungian, 129
juridical, iv, 99, 109, 118, 124, 131
jurisdiction, 100
justice, ii, 98-99, 112-113, 116-117, 126
justifiable, iv, 21, 53
justified, i
juxtaposition, 108

K

Kant, 6 n3, 14, 20 n15, 46 n25, 56 n28, 62 n30, 71, 82, 84 n41, 86 n45, 107, 110, 130
Kantian, 21 n16, 23 n17, 44, 75 n36, 81
kinesthetic, 77
knowable, 95, 101, 121
knowing, 20, 99, 108, 119
known, 1, 3, 11, 15, 18 n-24 n, 26, 33-34, 36, 38-40, 42-43, 45-46, 48, 53-56, 59, 61, 63, 67-68, 71-74, 76-80, 82, 84, 86, 89, 91-92, 105, 110-111, 116, 125

L

labours, 94
labyrinth, 1, 125
Lacan, 101, 103 n56, 114
lack, 86
landscape, 118, 121, 130
laws, ii-iii, vi, 55, 62, 80, 130
legal, 8
legalization, 66
legalized, 64
legislative, 109, 116
Leibniz' monad, 86 n
leitmotif, 127
lens, 3. *lex permissiva*, 85
liberties, iii
liberty, 67, 116
lifeworld, 126, 128, 131
lifeworlds, 129
lightning, 5
limitations, iv, 85, 96, 101-102, 111, 116-117, 122, 127, 130-131
limited, 61, 99, 101, 107, 115
limiting, 92
limitless, 2
limits, 9
linguistic, 113
literature, 106
localization, 77
localizing, 119
locked, 64
Logic, *The Science of* 82

logic, ii, v, ix, 9, 13, 69, 86 n45, 92-93, 97-98, 100-101, 106-107, 109, 111, 117
logical, 8, 21, 58, 61, 67, 73, 75, 105, 107, 109, 127
logos, 101, 103-104, 109, 124, 131
Lukács, 129

M

machinery, 5, 14, 49, 53-54, 81, 91, 93
machines, ix, 10, 12, 49, 54
Macro realism, v
made, iii, v, ix, 1, 7-8, 11, 26, 44-45, 54, 59, 61, 65, 67, 77, 83, 85-86, 91-92, 95, 103-104, 106, 108-110, 125-126
madman, viii
magazines, 125
magnetic, 4
magnifies, 26
Magnitude, 74
magnitude, 7, 9, 14-16, 19-20, 22-25, 29, 33, 35-40, 42-45, 53, 57, 66-67, 71-72, 74, 79, 82, 99
Magnitudes, 22, 38, 42, 82

magnitudes, 14-15, 19, 22, 38, 45, 50, 62, 74, 81-82
male, iii
management, 2, 9, 27, 30
mandate, 5, 30, 53, 64, 90
manifest, 95
manifestation, 69
manifestations, 95
manifold, 4, 12, 14, 16-17, 19, 33-34, 49, 52, 82-89, 91, 124, 130-131
manipulation, 15
manufacture, 52, 62
manufactured, 97
manufactures, 7, 30, 52
manufacturing, 4
marketplace, vii, 127
Martinus Nijhoffe, 68n
Marx, 102, 125
Marxist, 89 n49, 129
masculinity, ii
masse, 98, 100
masses, ii, 90
masterpiece, 127
masters, 13, 120
material, 21, 43, 46-47, 54, 65-66, 84, 90, 119, 123-124, 131-132
materialism, 83-84, 129
materialiter, 84 n41-85
materializes, 25
mathematical, 15, 48, 71
Matter-in itself, 21,24, 42-47,56, 43 n24
maverick, 11
mavericks, 99
maxim, 16, 88
maximized, 52
meaningful, vii
means, ii, 4, 11-12, 64, 84, 88-89, 96, 103, 106-108, 112-113, 121, 126, 132
measurable, 4
measured, 8
measures, 2, 4, 98-99
measuring, 48
mechanical, 6, 33, 48, 53
mechanics, 49
mechanism, 61
mechanisms, 3
mechanized, 53
Media, 65
media, 1-7, 9, 29-30, 51, 58, 61-62, 66-67, 69, 81-83, 90-91
medial, 61, 127
mediated, iv, 10, 110, 119
mediating, 9, 122, 132
mediation, 82 n, 122, 126
Mediations, 99 n54
meditations, 68n
medical, 85
Medieval, 104
medium, 58, 61, 78
mediums, 92
members, viii, 85, 91, 117, 119
memories, 2

men, iii
mental, viii, 23, 36, 129

merge, 14, 28, 69
merged, 27
merging, 25
message, v, 122
messaging, 67
meta-ontology, 125, -critical, 127
metaphor, 115
metaphysic, 31
Metaphysics, 25, 79, 84
metaphysics, 56
method, 4, 11
metonymic, 109, 115
metonymy, 115
microchip, 4
microphysical, 4
millennial horizons, 95 n52
millions(*in representation*), 90
minds, iii, vii, 6, 66, 90, 108, 111, 125
mirror, 22
mirrored, 23
misinformation, 10
mobility, 50
mobilize, 92
mobilized, 83, 132
modal, 56
modality, 9, 34, 47, 55-56, 124, 128, 131
mode, vi, 6, 16, 55, 61, 87, 106, 111, 115, 121
models, 10
modern, 3, 6, 65, 90, 95
modernity, v, 90
modes, 35, 55, 61, 115, 120
modified, 11, 71, 51
modulated, 79, 113, 115, 126, 132
modulates, 130
molecule, 49
moments, iv, 100, 104
momentum, 77, 79, 99
monad, 84, 86 n45
monadic, 84 n42
monadically, 85-86
monarch, 90
Monarchies, 106
monarchy, 90
monism, 56
monistic, 12
monitor, 104
monitored, 87, 101-102, 123
monster, 120
moral, 113
Morals, 84
morphic, 26, 28
morphological, 12, -*susbtrate*,16 n-17, -*representations* 25-26, 29,-*symbology* 71,
morphology, 24-28, 30
mortal, 131
motile, 130
motivated, 6, 8, 63, 93, 96, 109, 122
motivation, 2
motives, 107
motor, 49
motorcycle, 50
moulds, 108
movability, 27, 30, 49-50, 78
movable, 14, 49, 79, 100
movables, 14, 42, 65
moved, 63, 77-79
movement, 1, 5-6, 29, 56-57, 60-62, 64-65, 77, 98
movements, v, 92, 97, 105-106, 116
Multi-culturalism, 1
Multi-*functionality*, 35,-*dimensional*, 121
multiplicities, 100
multiplicity, 56, 83, 94-95
municipal, 66, 100

N

Narcissus, 22
national, 14, 27
nationality, 75
naturalism, viii
naturalization, 117, 119, 123
naturalize, ix
naturalized, ii, 6, 97, 105, 122
natured, 94, 130
natures, 113, 115, 118-119, 123, 128
necessitated, 62, 131
necessitating, 78
necessities, iii, 52, 58, 66, 110
Necessity, 1
necessity, iv, vi, viii, 22, 27, 57, 80, 91, 100, 124, 126
Negation, 34
negation, 18-19, 22, 68,132n
negationes, 16
negations, 12
Negative Dialectics, 101 n55

negative, i, 119-120
negotiation, 11
negotiations, 119
neo-Platonism, 4
neural network, 5, 8-10, 14, 59 n29, *of social ties*, 102, *-of projected noumenal beings*,17 n13
neurological, 9 n6
neurologically, 3
Newtonian, 61
nexus, 107, 109, 124
Nicomachean Ethics, 25 n
Nietzsche, 3 n2, 18 n14, 118-119
nightmares, 118
noematic, 114-115, 127-128, 131
noesis, 128
noetic,13, 87-90, 89n 102, 115, 126, 128, 130, 132
nominal, 114, 130-131
Non-being, 68
Non-binary, iii
nonsense, 112
normative, 122
normativity, 104
nothing, i-iv, vi-vii, 6, 13, 46, 66, 90, 93, 95, 103, 106, 119, 125-126, 131
nothingness, 66

Notion, *object*, (self-concept), 10, 17-18, 20-22, 24-26, 30, 34, 40, 42, 49-50,
Of value,83
Of essence, 85
Notionality, 30, 56, 58, 70, 75, 83
Notioned (*of its universality*), 25
Notions, 6
notions, 3, 6, 9, 13
Notre Dame Cathedral, 104
noumena, 22
noumenal,17 n, 47, 57, 114, 128
noumenon, 23
nuclear, 4, 81
nucleus, 1, 51
nutrition, 63
nutritive, 63

O

obfuscated, 102, 111, 113
obfuscating, 118, 126
obfuscation, 100-101, 104, 109, 130
Object, 17-18, 21, 24-26, 42, 49-50, 73, 82
object, 4, 7-8, 10, 12, 14-15, 17-25, 28, 30, 33-35, 37, 42-44, 49-50, 54-57, 60-61, 63, 67, 69-79, 81, 84-91, 94-95, 100, 102, 104-105, 107, 109, 114, 117-118, 121, 123-124, 126, 128
objectification, iv, 30, 45-46
objectified, 128
objectivation, 88
objective, iii, 56-57 61, 71-72, 85-88, 100-103, 109-110, 115-116, 119, 122, 125, 129, 131
objectively, 125, 131
objectives, 117, 123
objectivities, 102
Objectivity, 74
objectivity, 101, 103, 107, 117
objectness, 72
Objects, 33
objects, 3, 10-13, 17-22, 24, 26, 33-34, 40, 43-44, 47, 49, 52-55, 60, 62-63, 65, 67, 77-79, 84, 87-88, 100, 103, 105, 108, 110, 112, 114-115, 118-119, 125, 127, 130-131
obligation(s),53,85
observances, 110-111, 114-115, 128, 132
Occurrence, 31
occurrence, 1, 11-12, 22, 25, 29-33, 35, 50, 56-57, 71-72
occurrences, 5, 22, 29, 50, 55
October Revolution, 129

ontic, 15, 130, 132
Ontological, 1,10-11 (*ontico-*),15, 15-18n, 24,-30n,43n-44,46 52,*-field*, 56n

eplorations, 66,69

71, 77, 84n, 89, 91-92, 96, *-pre-*, Post-, 101,121,131, *-domain*,103, 107, 109, 113-116, 119, 121,123,*-transformation*,126, *-socio-*,127-128
Ontologically, 95
ontologically, 69, 127-128
ontologized, 47
ontology, 7-8, 12, 72, 122, 125, 128, 130
opened, 112, 120
opening(void), 102
operations, 4, 64, 119
opinions, viii, 99
opponent, 7, 20
opposed, 43, 100, 110-111, 115
opposing, 64
opposition, ii, iv, 78, 87, 95, 100, 119-121, 131
oppositions, 116, 120, 132
oppression, ii
oppressive, 117
oppressors, ii
optics, 3, 98
optimal, 54
orbit, 3
orchestrated, 11
ordered, 56, 96
ordinance, 3, 11, 16, 51, 66, 89
organic, 63-64
organicness, 63
organisms, 3, 51, 55
organization, 51
Organized, iii
organized, 94
originaliter, 84n, 86
origins, i, iii, 50, 52, 62, 96, 104, 107-108, 110, 112, 115, 123
Otherness, 111
otherness, 7, 16, 19, 23, 28, 42, 45-46, 68, 72, 88, 121, 124, 127
Others, 79, 102, 112
others, ii, 8, 52, 67, 79, 95, 109, 116-117
ousia, 79 n38, 111
outer, *regions of* thought, 100,*ontological experience,* 109
outposts, 9
output, 5
overlapping, 55
overshadowed, 129
overstimulated, 125
overstimulation, ix, 127
overthrow, v
overwrought, 113
ownership, vi-vii, ix, 65, 68, 117-118, 120
Own-essential, 85
ownness, 68, -essence, 85-86, 88 n47

P

pairing, 43 n24
paradigm, 3
paradigmatic, 7, 57
paradigms, 1, 5, 57, 83
paradox, 66
paralyzing, 6
paroxysm, 83
participants, v, 93, 95
participating, 29, 109, 111
participation, 116
particularism, 131
particularities, 99, 120, 124
particularity, 9, 27-28, 50, 60, 64, 69n, 84, 99n, 116, 127
particularization, 87
particularized, 126, 130
particulars, 3, 10, 23, 43
parties, iii, 11, 91
partisan, x
passage, v, 111
passengers, 125
passions, i, v
path, 53, 113, 126
paths, 119
pathway, 108
patience, 95
patient, 132
patterns, x, 53, 63
paying, iii, 96, 122
pays, 125
peaceful, vi, viii, 112
perceivable, 6-7, 19
perceive, v, 53, 82, 103, 114, 126, 128
perceived, ix-x, 11, 19, 23, 45, 49, 54-56, 79, 101, 105-106, 114, 116, 130
perceives, viii, 106, 121

perceiving, 88, 118, 121, 124, 127
perceptibility, 1
perception, vi, ix, 10, 12, 14, 19-20, 30, 32, 42, 44, 54-55, 61, 66, 87-89, 118, 121,
-*powers of,*123; 126
perceptions, 12, 22-23, 66, 92, 111, 130
perceptual, 6, 11, 14, 19-20, 64, 78, 83
perfection, iii, 54
perform, 13, 54, 67, 89, 98
performance, 4, 64, 106
performances, 122, 132
performative, 111
performed, 54, 103
performing, 63
performs, 48
periodicals, 1
periodicity, 71, 107
periods(*Ancient, Medieval*), 104
peripheral, i, 44
permanence, 65, 78, 84
permanent, 6
permissions, 85
perpetrators, vii
perpetuate, ii
perpetuated, 65, 125, 127, 129
perpetuating, 89
perpetuation, 120
perseverance, 132
persevere, 118
persevered, vi
persevering, 93
persist, 130
persists, 122
personal, 29, 66, 90, 95-96, 104, 112
personalities, 112
personality, 124
personhood, vi
persons, 9, 113
perspective, v, ix
perspectives, 97
perspicuity, 110
perversion, 5
perversions, 6, 66
petroleum, 48-49
Phenomena, 17
phenomena, 3, 12 n, 14-16, 18, 22-24, 26, 29, 31-33, 40,
43 n -45, 55-58, 61, 72, 75, 77-78, 92, 102-103, 105, 119-120, 126, 130
Phenomenal, 82
phenomenal, 3, 9, 15, 21-22, 25, 29, 45, 50, 57, 73, 75, 81-82, 84-85, 88-89
Phenomenological, 71
phenomenological, 1
Phenomenology, 69, 116
phenomenology, 87
phenomenon, iii-iv, 7, 20-24 n, 27, 32, 35, 43, 46, 74, 77, 119, 125
philanderers, 130
philology, 29
philosopher, 5
philosophers, 13, 74, 118
philosophic, 62, 113
philosophical, 5-6, 120, 129
philosophy, ix, 5, 90, 106, 112, 119, 122, 127, 129
photo, 63
photon, 4
physical, 15, 20-24, 84
physician, 52
physicians, 49
physionomy, 34
Picasso, 127
pitfalls, 52
pivotal, 116
plague, 53
planet, iv, vi, viii, 3-4, 51, 95-96, 103, 118-119
planetary, v-vii, ix, 106, 113, 126
plants, 3, 63
plateau, 80, 89n, 100
plateaus, 116
platform, 6
platforms, iii
Plato, 23, 131
Platonic, 14
Platonism, 4
plausible, 4
ploy, 20
plurality, 70, 121
polemical, viii
pollutant, 49
pools, 6
popular culture, 125

population, i, iii, vi, viii-ix, 2, 30, 51, 66-67, 90-91, 106, 118
populations, 67
populism, vii, 125, 127
populistic, ii
populous, 90
poses, 48, 53
posit, 11, 18-19, 49, 58, 83, 95, 113, 121
posited, i, 7, 12-13n, 22, 33-34, 42-44n, 46, 59, 62n, 66n, 70, 72, 78, 86, 88n, 91-92, 96 n53, 101-103, 109-112, 115, 117, 120-122, 124-132
positing, 1, 5, 44, 64-65, 71, 76, 78, 84 n, 114, 122, 126- *self*-,127, 132
positings, 106
positional, 103, 116, 124
positionality, 47, 101, 124
positioned, vi, 13, 21
positions, iv, vii, 46, 92, 95-96, 98, 113, 120, 125, 128, 132
posits, 6, 18-19, 22, 24-25, 36, 38, 40, 45-47, 61, 64, 69, 71, 74, 77, 81-82, 90, 99n, 110, 114, 121, 124, 128
possess, iv, ix, 19, 49, 53, 101, 103, 105-106, 108
possessed, vii, 54, 99, 108, 120, 123
possesses, v, 93, 116
possessing, ix, 24, 46, 113
possession, iii, ix, 4, 49, 88, 106, 116, 118, 124-125
possibilities, x, 5-6, 8, 15-16 n, 19-20, 35, 46, 49, 62-63, 66, 86, 95, 101-102, 106, 108, 114-115, 126-128, 131-132
possibility, 2, 7, 9, 16, 19-24, 35, 44-46, 60-63 n, 74, 80, 85, 95, 98, 100-101, 106, 108-110, 112-114, 119, 124, 132
Postmodern Enlightenment, 5
postmodern, i, vii-viii, 7, 127
postmodernism, v
potencies, ii, 105, 107, 123, 127
potency, vi, 97, 116, 130
potent, vii, 96, 129
potential, iv-v, 13, 53, 96, 106, 117
potentialities, 7, 86, 91-92
potentiality, 2, 8, 20-21, 29, 41, 46, 52-53, 56, 65, 82, 94
potentially, 79
powerful, 99
powers, ii, iv, vi, 9, 93, 101, 104-105, 108-109, 115-116, 118, 123
practices, 10, 51, 65-66, 95, 103, 108, 119
pragmatism, 64
praxis, 94 n51, 104
prayers, vii
precepts, 123, 129
precipitant, 52
precipitates, 70
precipitous, 50
precision, iii
preconceive, 102
precondition, 96, 124
predator, 63
predatorial, 64
predecessor, 72
predecessors, vii-viii, 98
predicable, 11, 15, 25, 37-39, 53, 71-72, 84
predicate, 26, 52
predicated, 26
predicates, 8
predication, 6, 11, 15-16
predicators, vii
predictability, 104
predicted, ix
predispositions, 52
preemptive, 130-131
prejudices, i
prerequisite, 80
presence, i, 5-9,

17-18, 20, 22, 25, 28-30, 44, 48-49, 53, 55, 58-59, 61, 63, 67, 72, 74, 77, 79-80, 90-91, 100, 110, 120
presences, 105, 123, 127-128
presentation, iv, 58, 68
presentations, 47
presented, 1, 3-4, 21, 23, 30, 43, 58, 61-62, 67, 72, 79, 112
presents, 4, 7, 22, 24, 54, 61, 65, 77, 80
preservation, 25-28, 90
preserve, 91
preserved, 78, 111
preserves, 90
pressures, 53
presumes, 57, 100
presuppose, ii-iii, 36, 101, 112, 114, 117, 122
presupposed, 90, 95-97, 99, 107, 111, 115, 125, 131
presupposes, 6, 36, 56, 67, 78, 87
presupposing, 9, 110, 131
presuppositions, 27, 101, 107, 114, 124-125
pretext, 123
prey, 63
primary, 4, 25, 27, 29
primitive, 2, 103
primordial, 88-91, 115, 119-120, 124, 128, 130
primordiality, 128
primordially, 91
Principium individuationes, 7, 86
Principle, first "" of predication, 6, Hegel's *negation of negation*, 18, 21-22, 25-31, 38, *of sufficient reason*, 69 *of universal information*, 69-70, 83
principles, iii, 6, 28, 84, 93, 129
priori, a, 6-8, 11, 16-22, 25-29, 33-36, 38, 42-44, 46, 55, 57-61, 72, 76, 80, 82, 86-91, 110, 124, 132
priority, 113
prisoners, ii
privation, 7, 53, 57-58, 64, 89
privilege, vii, 99, 112
privileged, ix
probe, 82
problems, ix, 54, 67, 88, 91, 93, 122
proclamation, i, 112
procreative, 122
produced, iii, ix, 48, 129
production, 102, 126
productive, 91, 96, 104, 109, 114, 126
productivity, 122
products, vii, 51
profession, 26-27
professional, 112
profit, 123
Pro-generative, 65
programmes, 99
programming, 2, 5, 83
programs, 3, 11
progress, ix, 2, 72, 94 96, 102, 104-107,109 118-119,125, 127
progressed, 107
progression, iv-v, ix, 2, 7-8, 13, 71, 118-120, 124, 130
progressive, viii, 6, 96, 102, 107, 117, 127-128
progressus, 8 n5, 11, 17, 36, 44-46, 72-75, 85-86
projected, 17, 23, 54, 64, 95, 107, 111, 118, 121, 127-128, 132
projecting, v, 110, 113, 130-131
projection, viii-ix, 21, 94-95, 99, 101, 105, 114, 116, 120-122, 124, 127-131
projections, x, 102, 116, 123, 132
projects, ii, 95, 126, 128 proliferating, ii, 131, proliferation, 30, promulgation, 96-97

propel, i-ii, 86, 100-101
propelled, i-ii, v, viii, 46, 95, 104-105, 107, 125-126, 130
propels, 66, 118
properties, 2-3, 5, 7-11, 13-15, 17, 26-28, 33-35, 43-45, 48-49, 52, 54-55, 60, 62, 65-66, 69, 72, 77-78, 81, 84-88, 92, 105, 120, 128
proponents, 105
proportion, 40, 48, 50, 96
proportional, iv, 1, 52
proportioned, 42, 52
proportions, i, 10, 48, 52, 54, 63, 66, 71, 84
proposed, iv, ix, 24, 101, 111, 120, 125
proposes, 34, 72, 74, 85-86
proposition, i-ii, 23-24, 42-44, 56, 84-87, 98, 123, 130
propositional, 69, 111
propositions, 45, 72, 87, 123-125
proprietary, 13, 48, 101, 105, 111-112, 115
proprieties, 66
propriety, 115
prospects, v, 93, 103, 105
prosperity, 113, 117
protected, 105
protectorate, vii
protectorates, iii
protocol, 27-28
providence, iv, 104
provincial, 27, 100, 119
provisional, 64, 84, 107, 117, 123, 125
provisions, 8, 81
provoked, vi, 110
proxies, 14, 17-18, 26
proximal, 8, 12, 15, 17, 26-28, 30, 60, 63, 77, 81, 84-85
proximate, 43, 87, 89
proximities, 9, 46, 52, 77
proximity, 9, 12, 14, 25, 28-29, 34-35, 40, 46, 58, 60-61, 65, 72, 81-82, 84, 89
proxy, 9-12, 14-18, 25-28
psyche, iii, v, 11-12, 14, 123, 125
psyches, vii, 54, 125, 129, 132
psychical, 6-7, 17, 110, 114
psychically, 54
psychoanalysis, 106, 117, 122, 129
psychoanalytic, 104, 129, 132 n63
psychological, 102, 106, 112-113, 115, 129
psychology, 106, 129
psychophysical, 84
psychosis, 117
psychotic, 132
publicness, 19
purchasing, ii, 117
pure, ii, iv, 22, 60, 63-64, 67, 83-84, 102, 107, 113
purposes, ii, viii, 2, 8, 55, 67-68, 71, 94, 105, 110, 116
purposive, 68, 79-80, 109
purposiveness, 10, 15-17, 25-28, 61, 80, 113, 132
pursuit, ii, v, 6-8, 10, 15, 17, 25, 46, 54, 64, 72, 83, 85, 113, 118, 120, 126
pursuits, viii, 16
purview, 124
puzzle, 54

Q

quagmire, 102
qualitative, 117, 120, 131-132
qualitive, 131
quantifiable, 84
quantifier, 119
quantifiers, 105
quantities, 70
quantity, 122
Quantum, 37, 82
quantum, 38, 131
quarrel, ix
quest, vii-viii, 64, 94, 101, 112

questions, vi, 90, 109
quotidian, 95, 114

R

racial, i
radiance, 53, 102, 113
radiant, 111
radiate, 100
radiates, 121
Radiation, 39
radiation, 4, 37, 39-40
radical, iv, viii,-*industrialization*, 3n, -*position*,7;13,71, 95, 105, 112-113, 116, 125-128
radically, 43n, 47, 74n, 115, 123
Radius (photon), 4
rain, 22, 56, 79
rainstorm, 56
Rational, 82
rational, 82, 84, 86, 93, 115
rationalism, 125, 127-128
rationality, 112, 120
rationally, 115
realism, v-vi, viii, 21, 127
realist, i, 19
realities, vi, viii, 54, 95, 104, 107
reality, i, iii-vii, 3n, 6, 45-46, 53, 62n, 84n, 93-94, 96-98, 100-101n, 103, 106-111, 113, 115-123, 125-126, 131-132
realization, iv, vii, 52, 114, 117, 129
realized, ix, 7-8, 18, 20, 22, 35, 43, 45, 53-54, 62, 64, 75, 81, 84, 90, 94, 99, 112, 121, 124
realm, 3, 6, 95, 108, 118, 122, 126, 128
reasonability, 113
reasonable, i, 95, 100, 105
reasoning, 86, 93
rebirth, 6
Reciprocity, 60
reciprocity, 18-19, 60, 64, 90
recognition, v, 62, 95, 108, 115, 121
recognizable, 124
recognized, 13, 110, 115, 118
reconcile, 90, 93, 104, 117, 124, 129
reconciled, 84
reconciles, 123
reconstitute, 64
reconstituted, 64
reconstitutes, 124
reconstruct, 102
records, 1
recovery, 27
recreated, 6
rectilinear, 21, 49
redeem, 6
redefine, 2
redesigned, 12
rediscovery, 13
reduced, 4, 102, 109
reducible, vi, 103, 105
reducing, 5
reductio ad absurdum, 27
reduction, 64
reference, 37, 48, 53
references, 66
referencing, 26
referent, 61
referential, 128
referents, 66
referring, 8, 23, 88-89
reflect, 53, 67, 90
reflected, 23, 131
reflection, 18, 22-25, 83, 86
reflections, iii, 111, 121, 125
reflective, 20, 23, 66, 94
reflexive, 1, 47-48, 69, 95, 102, 104, 108, 114, 120-121, 123, 127, 131
reflexivity, 115
reform, 117
refutation, iii
regenerated, iv
regime, 5, 131
regional, 100
regions, 95-96, 100, 108-109, 117, 128
regression, 107
regressus, 23n-24, 36, 42-46, 72-76n
regulate, iii
regulative, v, 110
Reich, *The Third*, 129
reification, 78, 129
reifications, 1, 67, 81
reified, 7, 58, 84, 95,

132
reifying, 103, 122
Relational, 60
relational, 15, 17, 22, 24-30, 52-58, 60-63, 69-70, 73-75, 78-79, 82-83 (beings, properties, objects)

relationality, 59, 76, 81
relationhood, 72, 83
relations, iv, 1, 4, 7, 9, 14, 17, 24-26, 33, 42, 44, 49, 57, 63-64, 83, 90-91, 105, 113, 120-121, 131
relationship, 90-91, 94, 103
relative, 11, 14, 29, 37-38, 44, 48-50, 52, 56-57, 61, 64-65, 70-71, 77, 79
relativist, 20, 70
relativity, 71
relevance, 58, 66, 71
relevant, 50, 131
relics, 106
religious, 104-105
remote, 3
renewed, iii, 63
renounce, 119
renounced, 74, 125
reoccurrence, 72
repair, iii, 54
repairs, 93, 99, 102, 125
repelled, i, 10, 23, 42, 95
repels, 21, 101
repetition, x
representability, iv, 112, 115, 120, 128, 131
representable, i, iii, 105, 116, 118, 121
Representation, *The World as Will and*, 7 n

representation, ii-iii, v, 3, 5, 8-10, 12, 15-28 n, 30, 35-36, 40-46, 54-61, 63, 65-67, 69-70, 72-81 n, 84-88, 90, 95-96, 100, 108, 113, 117, 119-120, 124, 127, 130
Representational, 35
representational, 11, 16-18 n, 21-22, 24, 26, 30, 47, 60, 69-70, 75 n-80, 89 n, 97
Representationality, 76
representationality, 76-77, 79
representationally, 59, 71, 90
representationed, 69
Representations, 22-23, 36, 56
representations, 1-7, 9-12, 14-18, 20, 23 n,-25, 28-29, 36, 41-44 n, 46, 55-57, 67, 69 n, 72-73, 79-81, 83, 94, 100, 102-104 n, 107-108, 110-113, 115, 127-128, 131
represented, 3, 26, 42, 52, 55, 59-61, 66-67, 77, 81, 86-89, 92, 96, 100, 121, 127
representing, x, 111, 123

represents, i, 17, 24, 50, 55, 59, 67, 79, 88
repressive, 102
reproduce, 59, 64, 119, 128
reproduced, viii, 63, 88
reproduces, 18
reproducibility, 127
reproducible, 102, 122, 127, 130
reproduction, ii, 28, 62-63, 66, 121
reproductive, 62, 104, 109, 114
residuum, 120, 129
resignation, 130
resigned, iv
resist, 119-120
resistance, vii, 108, 115, 117, 122
resolute, 5, 8, 13, 27, 107, 111, 121, 131-132
resolution, 27, 102
resolutions, 67, 98
resolve, iii-v, ix, 1, 10, 98, 127
resolved, ii-iii
resolves, 14, 25, 43, 61-62, 81
resolving, 10, 27, 85, 123

resonating, 93, 111, 115, 121, 123, 128, 132
resonation, 131
resounding, 111
resounds, 111, 124, 131
resourced, 107
resources, i-ii, v, ix, 28, 64, 92, 96
responses, ii, 48, 95, 122, 124
responsibilities, 92
responsibility, 53, 99, 116, 127

responsive, 5, 16, 22, 52, 57, 94, 100, 108-109, 114-115, 118, 124, 131
restrictions, 67
restructuration, v, 1
restructured, 2, 117, 128
restructuring, 112
resurgence, 105
reveal, 51-52, 71
revealed, 6, 51, 67, 116
reveals, iv, 28, 37, 44, 53, 57, 62, 72
revelation, ix, 72, 83, 121
revolt, 129
revolution, ii, vii, 9
revolutionary, 116, 130
revolutions, 13
rich, *in theory*, 90
riddles, 101
rift, 129
rights, v, 6, 84-85, 91, 100, 117
rigidify, 125
risk, 52, 100, 119
ritual, 52
rituals, 103, 116, 121
robs, 65
roots, viii, 112
rotates, 15
rotation, 15
rubber glove effect, 89
ruled, 110
rules, 10
ruling, 96
ruthlessness, 53

S

sacrifice, 52
sacrificed, 112, 125
sacrifices, 104, 113
sameness, 67
Sartre, 66 n31, 82 n39
satellite, 3, 7
satellites, 3
savage, 104, 113, 125
savants, 118
scandal, 2, 27
scene, 6, 102
schemata, 8, 28
schematization, 25
schematized, 70
schematizing, 70
scholars, 105
scholarship, 119
Schopenhauer, 3 n2, 7 n4,14, 21 n16, 23 n17, 43 n24, 46, n25 69 n33, 74 n35, 75 n36, 82 n39, 86 n45, 96 n53, 110, 118 n 61, 119
Sciences, 116
sciences, 64
scientific, 106
scission, 116
scope, iv, vii, 104, 113, 118
screen, 3, 15
screens, 3
scrutiny, 85, 123
search, 50, 82, 118-119, 125
searching, 104, 106
seclusion, 128
secret, 1, 4
sectors, 106
secular, 105
secured, 10, 64-65
security, i, 2-3, 9, 11, 51, 100
seduced, 100, 107
seeking, viii, 93, 118
selective, 25, 65
self-generating, 93
self-identification, 99n 104,132 *see* n63
Self-identity, 114, 118, 129
Self-realization, viii, 102, 107, 113
Self-regulating, 130
Sensation, 16, 24
sensation, 9, 12, 24-26, 42, 75, 89
senses, viii, 95
sensibility, 1, 9, 16, 74, 89, 113
Sensuous, 33
sensuous, 12, 34
sequences, 128
serenity, 53
series, 12, 23, 33, 36, 42, 46, 71, 125
server, 10, 14

servers, 9, 14
serving, 130
sexuality, 102
shadowed, 121
shadows, iii, 95, 106, 126, *of doubt*; Plato's 131
shallow, 99
shaping, 94, 103
sharing, 117
shelter, 79
shocking, ix
Shopping rituals, 103
shores, 93
shower, 56
showers, 79

significance, 10, 51, 53, 68, 71, 79, 95 n52,
significant, v, 2, 65, 71, 80, 88, 103-104, 112
signification, 59, 68, 72, 77-78, 104-105, 113, 119-120, 126, 130, 132
significations, v, 64, 69, 101, 107, 110-111, 115, 119, 121, 127, 131
signified, 1, 59, 64, 92, 100, 103-104, 114-115,118,124 126,131-132
signifieds, 119
signifiers, 12 n9, 100, 103 n56, 111-112, 114-115, 121-123, 129
signifies, v, 56, 76, 88, 123
signify, 78, 104, 113
signifying, 99, 101, 105, 132
signs, 18, 21, 23, 118
silence, 49, 103,108, *of one poor soul*,122

simplicity, 30, 101
simulacrum, 109, 114
singular, viii, 1, 4-5, 54, 80, 87, 95, 101, 115
singularities, vii
singularity, 8, 124
situation, ix, 11, 20, 44-46, 75, 82, 91, 124
situational, 11, 17, 21, 23, 25, 27, 35, 44, 60, 75-77, 82
situationality, 75
situations, iv, 100
Skull (Hegel), 43
socialized, 89
Socially,94
sociation, 119
societal, i, vi, 1, 30, 51, 64, 93, 104, 108, 113
societies, ii, iv-vi, viii, 53, 94
socio,-*cultural,*1, 3, 90, -*physical*, 84,116, -*ontological*,127-128
sociological, 90
sociology, 106
Socio-political, 97
Socratic, 131
software, 11-12, 15
solution, 67, 74, 89, 91
solutions, ix, 67
51-52
sophistry, 5
soul, i, iv, 6n, 57, 62, 64, 66, 83, 89, 93, 101-102,-*artificial* 118,-*mind-soul*, 121-122, 124
souls, viii, 54, 64, 99, 104, 108
source, ii, 6, 10, 30, 52, 59, 62-63, 66, 75, 84, 88, 93-94, 112, 120, 123
sourcehood, 9, 43
sources, i, 9, 51, 129-130
Soviet Space Program, 3 n1
Spaces, i-iv, 55, 112,-*of representation*, 116, 118, 121, 127-128
spatial, 12, 21-22, 24, 44-46, 58, 105
spatiality, 12, 58
spatialization, 77
species, iv, vii-ix, 28, 30, 51-55, 62-65, 89, 91, 94-95, 98, 112, 126
specifically, 67, 105
specified, 3, 71
spectre, i
spectrum, 78

speech, 96, 101, 103
sphere, 28
spheres, 62
Spinoza,5,12 n,56 n , 132
spirit, i, iv, 65, 94, 111, 116, 126 spirits, v, 93, 108,

119
spiritual, 53, 101, 108, 113, 117, 119, 121-122
sport, *never hunting for*, 63
starlight, 93
stasis, 62, 79

states, i, vi, viii, 38, 42, 91, 98, 119, *symbolic* (etc.) 130
stations, 94
status, vi-vii, 28, 90, 120, 130
stoics, 50
storms, 55
strata, 83, 87-91, 126
stratification, 13, 82, 88
stratifications, 65, 96, 116, 126
stratified, iv, 8, 17 n13, 95
stratospheres, 95
stratum, 89n, 91, 115, 132
stream, 9-10, 15
streams, 8 strength, 54, 118 structural, 25, 101, 116-117, 119, 128
structuralist, 99
Structuralists, 115
structuration, 132
structured, 57, 110
structures, 8, 25, 29-30, 95, 104, 107, 127 struggle, iv, 64, 75 Sub-code, 4, 10-11 subjective, iii-iv, 6,18,47,74-75 88-89, 96, 99-104, 109-111, 114-115, 117, 119, 122-124, 130-132
subjectively,-posited 44,-ratified (Descartes) 125
subjectivism, 102

subjectivities, 75
subjectivity, iii, *insofar as being is primary to*, vi-vii, 18n, 21n, 27, 43n, 75n, 79n, 87n, 94n-96, 100-103n, 107-108, 111-112, 115, 117-118, 120-121, 123-127, 129, 131
subjects, vii, ix, 7, 14-15, 27, 57, 65, 67, 87-89, 98, 101-102, 105, 108-109, 115-116, 118, 126, 128-130
subjugate, 67
subjugated, 122
subjugation, 98
sublimated, 107
sublimity, 126
submerged, 27, 132
subordinate, 98, 107, 126-127, 129
subordinated, 69, 103, 111, 127
subordination, 109, 111, 128
subordinations, 123, 132
subservience, 96
substance, 78
substances, 24, 48, 84
substrate, 3, 12, 16, 18, 24-25, 29-30, 70, 77, 81, 89-90, 102
substratum, 16, 24, 34, 81, 85, 88,90-91

Sugars(photosynthesis), 63
suicide, 52
Supersession of forms, 100
superstructures, 29-30, 38
superficiality, 113,125

superimpose, 110
superior, 49, 51, 91
superposes, 85
superposition, 115
superscope, 23
supersede, 27, 85, 94 superseded, 27, 59 supersedes, 8, 28, 30,106
supersession, 100
superstition, 110
superstructure, 2-3, 5 superstructures, 7, 30 supervenience, 27,83,85
supervenient, 8, 58, 64, 66
suppressing, 67
Supra-temporal, 87
survival, vii, 63-65, 89-90
survive, 90, 107
sustain, 46, 91, 106, 122
sustainability,100, 123,sustainable ,55,
sustained, 98

symbol, i
Symbolic, 98, 121
symbolic, i-ii, v, vii, 43, 67, 93, 96 n,97, 99-100, 102, -dimension, 103 n, 111, 112-124, 126-132 n
symbolically, iv, 106, 110-111, 116, 125, 127-128
symbolism, vii
symbolization,18n14, 21 n16, 100-101, 103-106, 109-110, 118, 120-121, 128, 130
symbolizations, 107, 111
symbolized, 102
symbolizes, 123
symbology, 71
symbols, 100, 103-106, 108, 110, 113
symptoms, 132
Synchronic representations, 73
synchronicities, 118
synchronicity, 11-12, 45, 71
synchrony, 72
synecdoche, 115
synonymous, 52
syntactical, 96, 114, 119, 124, 131
syntheses, 120
synthesis, iii-iv, 10-11, 16, 24, 55, 62-63, 69-71, 80, 86-87, 107, 119-120
synthesize, 52
synthesized, 69
Synthetic, 9n-10, 17, 20, 22-23, 34, 44, 55, 61, 69-71, 84, 86-87, 98, 107, 126, 131
synthetical, 110
synthetically, 3, 17, 71, 99
systematic, 12, 53
systemization, 82
systemized, 7
systems, 1, 3-4, 7, 9-10, 12, 28-30, 48-49, 51, 64, 78, 83, 89-90, 120, 126

T

tables, 125
targets, i
tears, 57
Tech-genera, 25-26, 28, 69-70
Techno-(etc.), 16-18
technocracy, 91
technocratic, 5, 7
technocrats, 1, 4, 9
Technological, 60, 93
technological, v, 1-5n, 7-9n, 10-16nn, 18n,28n-29, 35, 53-54, 58-59, 61-62, 64, 69-71, 73, 75, 80-81, 90-92, 95n
technologically, 1-2, 8, 59, 61, 69
technologies, 1, 3-4n, 17n, 52, 54,media, 66, 94n
technologize, 2
technologized, 15, 17, 65, 69
technologizing, 4, 91
Technology, 48, 69
technology, viii, 2, 4-5, 8-9, 12n, 14, 16-17, 25n-26, 28, 30, 35, 53, 58-59, 61-62, 69, 80, 95, 97, 122
teeth, 112
teleological, 24, 119
teleology, 30, 63
telephones, 3
Televised media, 3
televisions, 3
template, 5, 16, 25
temporal, 19, 57, 69-72, 77-78, 87, 107, 114, 130
temporality, 12, 23, 55-57, 66, 69, 71, 77-79, 85, 107
temporalization, 16, 45, 103
temporalized, 10, 12, 43, 45, 69
temporally, 70
terminal, 9-10, 12, 14-15, 17-18, 24, 27-28, 52, 83-84
terminality, 28
terminals, 10, 14, 16-17
terrain, 13, 91n, 94, 107, 109, 115-117, 119, 122, 124, 128
text, 9-10, 15
themselves, *beings-in ,etc.*,14-16, 18-19, 22, 24, 30, 38, 43-44, 46, 55-58,

67, 72-74, 77-80, 82-87, 95, 98, 100, 103, 110-111, 115, 122, 129-131
theocracy, 111
theoretical, 92, 127
Theoretically, 49
theories, 13
Theory of a Novel, 129
thermodynamics, 48
thermological, 48-50
thief, 113
thieves, 112
Thing-in-itself,10, 20 n15,23,30,58, 77,82,102,126-127
thingness, 75
Things, 59, 72, 77
things, 6, 8, 12, 15, 18, 22, 30, 38, 44, 50-51, 53, 55-58, 62-63, 74, 78-82, 84-87, 96, 98, 100, 103-106, 108-111, 113-114, 119-120, 123, 130
Things-in-themselves, 7, 10, 77
thinkers, 118, 129
thinking, 91, 95, 129
thirties, nineteen-, ix
thoughts, 5, 93, 95, 101-103, 107-108, 125
threat, 48, 54, 85
threshold, 69
thresholds, 108
Tinman, 50
tool, 94
tooled, 51
tools, 4, 30, 79
totalities, 1, 128
totality, iv, viii, 2, 6, 11-12, 14-15, 17, 27, 42, 44, 51-52, 56, 66-69, 72, 74, 77, 88, 90-92n, 94n, 96, 98, 100-101, 103n, 106-108, 111, 113, 115, 122, 126-127, 130-132
totalization, 74n, 114, 117, 129-130
totalize, 105
totalized, 77, 115
totalizing, 122
Tracked *by a corporate entity anywhere*, 3

trading, 66
traditions, 95, 125
tragic, 50, 128
tragical, 128

transaction, 11
transactions, 64
transcend, v, vii, 52, 64, 94, 98, 122, 126-127, 130, 132
transcended, 103, 111, 122, 124

Transcendence, 93
transcendence, i, 66n, 83-87, 95n, 97, 99-103n, 106-113, 118, 121, 124, 126, 130
transcendences, 46, 130
transcendency, 116
transcendent, 36, 66, 85, 92, 102, 124
Transcendental, 83, 116
-aesthetic, 21 n16
83, 85-87, 110, 128, 131
transcending, 96, 104, 108, 115, 117, 126, 128
transcends, 110, 117, 119, 123
Transference, 97
transferred, 12, 26, 93, 98, 124-125
transferring, 94
transform, 94
transformation, ii, v-vi, viii-ix, 1, 13, 59, 85, 92, 106,*social*, *ontological*, *empirical* 110, 112, 115, 126-128, 130
transformative, 99, 121, 124
transformed, 125, 127-128
transforming, 122
transforms, iii
transgressions, 123
transition, viii, 128
transmission, v, vii, -*symbolic*, - *neuronal*, 12, 14, 94
transmit, 3
transparent, 98
Trans-positional, 124
traps, 94
traumatic, 102
treasures, 118
treatment, 132
trends, 103
tribute, 125
trigger, 125
troubadours, 99
troughs, 93, 101, 108, 123
truism, 44

Truth, 45-46
truth, i, iii-vi, 1-2, 8-9, 11, 17-24, 28-30, 35, 42-46, 56-57, 66, 68, 75-76, 81-84, 86, 93, 96, 98, 100-104, 106, 108, 113, 115, 118-122, 125, 127
twenties, *nineteen-*, 4

U

unconditional, 45, 120
Unconditioned, 44-45, 62, 72, 75
unconditioned, 17, 23-25, 36, 44-46, 59-60, 62, 73-74, 78, 86, 92
unconscious, 96, 129-130
unconsciously, 2, 5
undermine, vii, 119, 123
undermined, 115
undermines, 97, 118
understanding, ix, 9, 22-23, 30, 51, 54, 62-63, 69, 84-85, 91, 104, 106, 111, 115, 124
undisclosed, 108
undivided, 94
unethically, 117
unforeseen, 2
unhindered, 127, 130
unification, 9, 100-101, 115, 128
Unified, 131
unified, 19, 24, 56, 80, 100, 111
uniform, ii, v
uniformity, 19, 100, 130
unify, 120
unifying, 100-101
unintelligible, 120
unities, 55
unity, 10, 17, 22, 34, 44, 55-58, 69, 78, 110
Universal, 8, 16, 28, 64
universal, i-ii, v-viii, 1, 8, 10, 24, 28n,29, 49, 69-70n, 83-85, 87, 94, 99, 101, 105, 115-116n, 124, 126, 130-131
Universality, 6-7, 10, 16, 62, 65
universality, viii, 25, 29, 49-50, 66, 69, 97, 99, 112, 119, 126, 130-131
universalization, 75
universalized, 69, 97, 115-116n, 123
universally, i, 45, 69, 85
universals, 8-9, 66 n
universe, v, 10, 62, 71, 105
unjust, 99
unknown, 50, 67
unlivable, viii
unmediated, vi, 10, 119
unnecessary, 1
unnoticed, ix
unpredictability, 54
Unravel (*mystery of matter-in-itself*), 24
unreasonable, 102, 104
unregulated, viii
unrest, vii
unsustainable, 55
upheaval, 125
Uranium, 4
user, 10, 15, 17
using, 9, 23
utility, 21, 65-66, 94
utilize, 55
utilized, 3, 11, 23, 48-49, 63, 74, 94, 104
utilizes, 5

V

valuation, 1, 64, 127
valued, v
vanities, 94, 132
variability, 75 n36, 78, 104, 112, 119-120
variable, 78, 106
variables, 50
varying, ii, 52
vegetation, 63
vehicle, 9, 49
vehicles, 49
veiled, 5
velocity, 37-39
vengeful, i
ventilation, 48
verifiability, 109, 111
verifiable, 96, 110
verifiably, 119
verification, 85-86, 88
verifying, 98
verisimilitude, 109

Verneinung, 132n
Vertical
consciousness, 89n,
91n, 115
viability, 96, 99, 109
victimized, 91
victorious, 98
violate, 57
violation, 91
violations, 116
violence, 53
virtual, 9, 11, 58-59,
128
Virtualities, 59
virtualities, 59n
virtuosity, 10
visibility, 95-96,
98-99, 130
visible, 23n, 63, 96,
122
vision, i, 98, 118-119
visions, 6
vital, viii, 96, 101,
107
vitality, 53, 113, 130
vituperation, 27
voice, 120
void, 16-17, 102,
124, 126, 130
vulnerable, 6, 108,
130

W

walls, 120-121, 126
wanderlust, 105
warning, 55
wars, iii
wasteful, viii
wealth, 65
weaponry, 81
weighted, 1, 11, 14,
64
Well-represented, 94
Western -*civilizations* , viii,- *thinking*, 129
WikiLeaks, 27 n 21
wilderness, 121
willing, vii, 99, 111,
113, 127, 132
wills, 6, 8, 10,
14-16, 22, 45, 54,
96, 99, 114, 116,
125, 127
wiped, 2
wired, 9
wires, 2
wisdom, 59, 93, 95,
101, 115
wishes, ii, vii, 5, 53,
94, 123
witness, iv, 52
Wittgenstein, 103
Wolfman, iv
working, 1, 9, 27, 51
works, 1, 15, 26
world, 116
worldwide, 122
wounds, iii
wreckage, 91
WWII, 4

Y

Y2K scare, 2
years, iii, 4, 13, 93,
103
yesteryear, 95

www.ingramcontent.com/pod-product-compliance
Lightning Source LLC
Chambersburg PA
CBHW032256150426
43195CB00008BA/474
* 9 7 8 1 7 7 5 2 8 4 8 7 1 *